WE ALL SHINE ON

WE ALL SHINE ON

JOHN, YOKO, AND ME

ELLIOT MINTZ

DUTTON

DUTTON

An imprint of Penguin Random House LLC
penguinrandomhouse.com

Photographs on pages ii, 201, and 203 by Nishi F. Saimaru, courtesy of Ms. Saimaru and the author.
Photograph on pages 13 and 15 © Bob Gruen/www.bobgruen.com. Photograph on pages 79 and 81
courtesy of the author. Photograph on pages 147 and 149 by Richard Creamer/Michael Ochs Archives.

LIBRARY OF CONGRESS CATALOGING-IN-PUBLICATION DATA
Names: Mintz, Elliot, author.
Title: We all shine on: John, Yoko, and me / Elliot Mintz.
Description: [1.] | New York : Dutton, 2024. | Includes index.
Identifiers: LCCN 2024031239 | ISBN 9780593475553 (hardcover) |
ISBN 9780593475560 (ebook)
Subjects: LCSH: Lennon, John, 1940–1980. | Ono, Yoko. |
Lennon, John, 1940–1980—Friends and associates. |
Ono, Yoko—Friends and associates. | Mintz, Elliot. | Beatles. |
Dakota, The (New York, N.Y.)
Classification: LCC ML420.L38 M57 2024 |
DDC 782.42166092/2—dc23/eng/20240705
LC record available at https://lccn.loc.gov/

Printed in the United States of America

1st Printing

BOOK DESIGN BY KRISTIN DEL ROSARIO

To John, Yoko, and Sean

CONTENTS

CONTENTS

The Dakota, February 1981

I am holding in my hands a pair of eyeglasses. They are antique, made of steel wire, and perfectly round. Some people used to call them granny glasses, although this pair's trademarked name is the Panto 45, originally manufactured by an old English eyewear company called Algha Works.

I don't have it in me to try them on—that would somehow cross a line—so instead I just hold them up to my eyes and peer through the lenses from arm's length. But even without slipping them onto my nose, they tell me something about John Lennon's view of the world that I'd never really thought much about while he was alive.

His vision was terrible—even worse than I'd ever thought.

This is the twenty-sixth pair of John's glasses I've examined on this snowy night in February 1981. It's been about two months since he was gunned down in New York City outside the Dakota, the now 140-year-old brick-and-sandstone Gothic edifice on West Seventy-Second Street and Central Park West where he and Yoko Ono had been living since 1973. I've been tasked with the responsibility of inventorying his personal effects—books, wallets, attaché cases, drawings, letters, artworks, photos, musical instruments, and, yes, granny glasses, of which he had dozens of pairs in a rainbow of tinted colors—so that Yoko, and posterity, would know precisely what he had left behind.

Most of this heartbreaking work, which fills weeks of my life, is performed between midnight and six in the morning—the hours during which I am least likely to be disturbed by the small army of assistants and other staffers who buzz around John and Yoko's multiple apartments at the Dakota, much of it taking place in the building's crypt-like sub-basement. It's the dead of winter and there's no heating in this underground catacomb, which once served as the Dakota's stables back when New York was a horse-and-buggy town but which in more recent years has been converted into storage stalls for its well-to-do tenants. It's so cold and dank, I can see my breath as I sift through John and Yoko's vast collection of artifacts. My fingers are numb as I jot down descriptions of every item I can identify in a growing series of notebooks that will eventually be transcribed and printed into two five-hundred-page bound volumes.

I did not ask for this task. I certainly did not want it. For one thing, I live 2,500 miles from the Dakota, in Los Angeles, where

I host a late-night radio interview show. Taking stock of John's possessions means multiple cross-country trips, which even for a relatively young man like me—I'm in my mid-thirties at this point—can get pretty exhausting.

But Yoko asked me to do it, and I have rarely been able to say no to Yoko, let alone John. It was, in fact, the story of my life, doing what John and Yoko asked of me. If only I *had* learned to say no—if only I'd had the strength to resist the undefinable magnetic pull both of them had on me for so many years, starting almost from the very moment, in 1971, when we first met on my radio show—I might have discovered a very different destiny for myself. I might have ended up living a more balanced, traditional existence. I might have married, had children, or even made some ordinary friends who didn't hold extraordinary secrets I had to keep from the prying eyes of the entire world.

If friends are even the right word for John and Yoko.

THE English language contains some 170,000 words, and yet I've never come across a single one of them that fully describes the odd contours and strange angles that made up my relationship with John and Yoko. Over the nine years that I spent with John before his death—and the forty more with Yoko afterwards—I played many parts in the sometimes puzzling, occasionally maddening, always complex dramas they scripted for the three of us. I was a trusted confidant, a fixer of problems, a media rep (although I was never officially employed by either until after John's death), an investigator, a sounding board, a traveling mate, a connection to the outside world, a sometime babysitter (not for their young son, Sean, but for John, who tended to need one more), and, above all else, a 24-7 tele-companion who spent literally hundreds of hours on the phone with them in epic transcontinental conversations that could go on for six or seven hours at a stretch.

I knew how I felt about both John and Yoko: I loved them like family. I'd like to say they felt a similar familial attachment to me—I hope they did—but, again, I was never completely sure what their true feelings were. All I knew was that when they called—which they did constantly—I felt compelled to answer. In the years we were together, nobody spoke with them more than I did. I'll never know exactly why mine was the number they so frequently dialed, but I know I always did my best to be a true friend to them both. Even at the most challenging times, I was there for John and Yoko, refusing to take sides, telling them truths that could sometimes be hard to hear. They trusted me, and I trusted them in return. It was a relationship and re-sponsibility that was almost always a joyous one. But for the past few months, it's been a heavy one.

At this moment, in February 1981, at Yoko's request, the function I am performing in the middle of the night is archivist and scrivener.

I am performing it with robot-like dispassion, or at least as close to it as I can muster. It's the only way I can handle the horror of the job, the finding and examining—the *touching*—of John's left-behind belongings, all that remains of the man who for so long had been at the center of my world and of my heart.

As agonizing as it is, though, it is vital work. In the days and weeks after John's death, I spend a lot of time in New York helping Yoko deal with the logistical fallout of his murder: talking to the press, the police, and the swarms of opportunists who suddenly descend upon their estate. As I bustle about their apartments—they owned two massive units on the Dakota's seventh floor, as well as several others dotted around the building—I begin to notice that some of John's effects are disappearing. Not the overtly valuable stuff, nothing that would draw much attention, but small personal items that wouldn't immediately be missed. For instance, John kept a small cassette player and radio on a night table in their bedroom so he could listen to music or lectures. One day, it simply isn't there any longer.

I begin to suspect that a thief is among us.

These minor larcenies are, I suppose, predictable: anything John possessed or even merely touched is imbued with extraordinary financial value, especially since his death. A simple doodle he might have scratched out on a notepad could suddenly be worth a great deal of money. Other more meaningful items—like, say, the five volumes of his personal diaries he kept hidden under his bed—would obviously be priceless beyond measure, which we would later learn the hard way when they actually *were* stolen. Understandably, Yoko doesn't want John's belongings bartered on the black market, which is one of the reasons she asks me to catalogue everything I can find that he owned.

And so I adjust the wool scarf around my neck, which does little to ward off the damp, bone-chilling air in the Dakota basement, and continue my work. The lighting here is terrible and the flickering of the fluorescent bulbs dangling from the ceiling is giving me a headache. The Dakota is a beautiful old Renaissance Revival–style building, but it is, frankly, a bit foreboding—it's no accident that Roman Polanski chose its exteriors for Mia Farrow's apartment in *Rosemary's Baby*—particularly late at night and especially in these dungeon-like lower floors. After three or four hours, I decide I've had enough. I gather my notebooks and head to the old elevator that will carry me back to the warmth and relative comfort of the seventh floor, where I'll continue my late-night cataloguing by opening every door, drawer, and cabinet I can find in John and Yoko's sprawling apartments.

In one closet, I discover some of John's old costumes: the ornate British Army–inspired uniform he wore on the cover of the *Sgt. Pepper's Lonely Hearts Club Band* album and the Chesterfield suit he and his fellow band mates were garbed in during their first appearance on *The Ed Sullivan Show*. I write them down in my notebooks. In another apartment there is a group of black steel filing cabinets where I find a folder packed with old love notes to Yoko written while John was studying with the Maharishi in India, and another filled with scores of old Polaroid photos. (John was an early adopter of instant photography, shooting some of the world's first selfies, including, for some reason, many of his own feet.) Those I catalogue as well.

Some of the items I uncover seem to me bizarre, even alien. For instance, I have no idea at first what to make of the sawed-in-half furniture I find in the basement—half a chair, half a table—as well as an all-white chess set with all-white pieces. It's only later that I learn that these objects had been part of several of Yoko's art exhibits, including her famous *Half-A-Wind Show* at the Lisson Gallery in West London in 1967.

In an unsecured room in one of their apartments, I find John's priceless collection of guitars. I count them all—including a Rickenbacker 325, a Yamaha Dragon, a Gibson J-160E, a Fender Telecaster, and an Ovation Legend—and jot them into my notebook. (Later, I'll slip a note under Yoko's bedroom door urging her to add a more robust lock to the room.)

During one especially memorable excavation, I stumble upon cardboard boxes filled with hundreds of cassette tapes containing hours of never-before-heard recordings: John taping himself at the piano as he teased out the music to some of his most famous tunes; his musings as he worked through the lyrics, rehearsal recordings, and acoustic songs in varying stages of development; interviews, lectures, and some of John's recollections of his childhood in Liverpool, presumably for an autobiography that he never got around to writing. Years later, with Yoko's permission, I'll broadcast many of these historic recordings in a 219-episode weekly radio show, *The Lost Lennon Tapes*. It will air nationally on the Westwood One Radio Network and millions will tune in to what may well be the world's very first (and certainly longest) bonus track.

My central headquarters while undertaking this massive cataloguing operation is a bedroom in the main residence. In fact, it's the very bedroom where John and Yoko slept and spent most of their lives together in the Dakota, and where I would sometimes sit with them, slouched in a white wicker chair by their bed—a large mattress on a slab of plywood resting on two vintage church pews—whiling away long nights in discussions about everything from history to metaphysics. For obvious reasons, Yoko now avoids the space; she moved into another bedroom after his murder. That is the very reason I choose it as my home base for this assignment. Once their private inner sanctum, it's become a nondescript, little-visited guest room, the most secluded spot on the seventh floor.

Yoko has had most of the bedroom furniture removed, although, for reasons she never explains, she leaves my wicker chair in the corner, where it's always been. It's odd to see such a familiar area stripped so coldly bare, but I quickly fill the room with desks and other office fixtures. I install VHS cameras, microphones, tape recorders, and a slew of monitors, turning the bedroom into a home audio-video studio designated solely for the purpose of conducting the inventory. I want to make absolutely sure that I document my work visually and audibly throughout the cataloguing process, so every single item I find is eventually brought into this room and captured on tape. I'm aware that my diligence in this regard is raising eyebrows among some of Yoko's staffers—they think I'm going dramatically overboard—but I believe it is essential that this process be flawlessly transparent, especially considering all the possessions that have already gone missing since John died.

On this particular blizzardy night in February, it's so quiet in the bedroom turned studio, I can practically hear the snow falling outside the window. I sit down in the wicker chair and rub my weary eyes, thinking about what I've found over these long hours, particularly, for some reason, John's many pairs of eyeglasses. When I peered through them, I got to see the world through John's highly myopic eyes, and now I can't help but consider the possibility that his terrible eyesight might have been one of the keys to his genius. Perhaps his blurry view of the world allowed him to see the universe with a lucidity that eluded better-sighted mortals. Maybe he perceived a side of reality—beautiful, surreal, and fantastical—that was hidden to those of us cursed with 20/20 vision.

But then, out of the edge of my own eyes, I spot an object in the room, tucked away in a corner, that snaps me out of my musings. It's something I usually go out of my way to ignore, something I have been avoiding dealing with for weeks, since the day representatives from Roosevelt Hospital delivered it to the Dakota, handing it over as gingerly as fine crystal. It's a twin-ply paper bag, folded at the top and heavily stapled. Inside are the clothes John was wearing the day he was killed—a pair of pants, a black leather jacket, a blood-soaked shirt, and, hauntingly, a pair of blood-spattered eyeglasses—along with a few items he was carrying in his pockets.

I do not catalogue these items. I cannot bring myself to open the bag, let alone videotape what's inside. In fact, I deliberately pretend it's not there. But on this night, for reasons unknown, I allow myself to stare for a second or so too long. It's a big mistake.

The bag plunges my imagination into dark, twisted places. Although I was a continent away the moment John was murdered, puttering around my small house in Laurel Canyon, I can see in my mind's eye his final moments. I visualize the assailant, the deranged twenty-five-year-old *Catcher in the Rye* fan turned murderer, as he takes a combat stance and fires his Charter Arms .38. I imagine how the illegal hollow-point bullets he had acquired ripped through John's body, tearing parts of his torso to shreds. I can hear the sounds of Yoko's screams, the shattering of glass, the thud of John's face hitting the hard pavement as he stumbled to the ground.

I wallow in these nauseating visions for way too long, unable to shake them from my head as I stare at that stapled bag in the corner. Like a tragic character in an Edgar Allan Poe story, I'm all but mesmerized by this telltale sack of horrors—until, after who knows how many minutes, I somehow notice that the heavy brass knob on the door to the bedroom is slowly turning. I stare at it as it moves bit by bit, almost imperceptibly, like in a scene from a classic noir movie thriller. This is extremely unusual. Nobody ever comes into this room anymore except for me, certainly not at this late hour. I sit up straight, my heart starting to race, watching as the door begins to open in what seems like slow motion.

In the darkness of the hallway, I can't quite make out what it is. At first, I wonder if it's a child: the silhouette is tiny, barely a whisp of a person. For a second, I entertain the notion that it's a ghost. The Dakota has a long history of hauntings; the poltergeist of a long-dead young girl bouncing a ball in its hallways has been reported on multiple occasions, once by John himself. But then she takes a step into the room.

"Hello, Elliot," she says in a soft whisper.

She looks nothing like the Yoko you've seen in magazines or on television, the edgy, avant-garde artiste with the wraparound sunglasses. She's wearing a housecoat and slippers, her long black hair is a tangled mess, and she seems even more diminutive than usual. Since John's death, she's hardly been eating; she's so thin and frail, it's alarming. And while, like me, she's always been something of a nocturnal animal, she hasn't been sleeping much, either, which may explain why she's wandering around the seventh floor at four in the morning looking like an actual apparition.

"Hello, Yoko," I respond after I regain my composure. "Are you okay?"

Her expression, which has never been particularly easy to read, is almost completely blank. She stands at the doorway for the longest moment, surveying the room, until her gaze finally settles in my general direction. Part of me wants to rush up to her to give her a hug—she really looks like she could use one—but Yoko is not remotely a hugger. She is rarely demonstrably affectionate.

"No," she says, "I don't need anything, Elliot."

There's another long pause while we silently, awkwardly stare at each other.

"Yoko?" I finally ask her. "Can I get you anything?"

She lets slip the barest hint of a grin. "I just wanted to say hello," she says.

Then she steps back out the door into the dark hallway, leaving me alone to ponder, as I have so often in the years I've known her, the enigma of Yoko Ono's smile.

PART ONE

PLEASE
PLEASE ME

ONE

Laurel Canyon, 1970

Once upon a time, there was a place called Laurel Canyon. It's still around, of course. Turn north off Sunset onto Laurel Canyon Boulevard, steer up the hill for about a mile, past the Canyon Country Store, and you'll wind up in a neighborhood that continues to go by that name.

But it's not Laurel Canyon. Not the Laurel Canyon I knew back in the 1970s.

Every couple of decades or so, certain geographical points become epicenters of creativity, inspiration, and invention. Paris in the 1920s. Chicago in the 1930s. New York in the 1950s. And in the 1970s, the spot on the planet that seemed to magnetically attract the world's best and brightest artists, especially in the music industry, was this deceptively quiet enclave nestled like a secret garden between the San Fernando Valley and what was then the wheezing heart of old Hollywood.

When I moved to the neighborhood in the late 1960s, I had no idea what I was about to experience. I was a young broadcaster in my twenties, bouncing from job to job at various L.A. radio stations, collecting unemployment checks between gigs, and I needed a cheap place to live. At the time, Laurel Canyon was the city's bohemian district, poor cousin to Benedict and Coldwater Canyons, which were closer to ritzy Beverly Hills. The modest two-story house I ultimately settled into on Oak Court— then a dead-end dirt road—cost me all of $300 a month. It was tiny, maybe nine hundred square feet, with a kitchenette barely big enough to boil an egg, and it was perched so high up on the edge of a steep slope you had to climb a mountain of rickety steps to get to it. Fortunately, the landlord had installed a "hillevator"—a sort of open-air electric tram—that shuttled you from street level to the house's front door. Or at least, it did when it was working.

What drew me to the area—aside from its affordability—was its charming rustic ambiance. It was a short five-minute drive up the hill from the Sunset Strip, which even back then was a honking, teeming hive of urban activity. But once you got to the top of the road, you suddenly found yourself in a magical forest enveloped under a canopy of elderberry and eucalyptus trees. A mile below, it was traffic lights, fender benders, exhaust fumes, and police sirens. Up here, it was hummingbirds, butterflies, and bunnies, a pastoral sanctuary where the calming scent of jasmine (and oftentimes marijuana) perfumed the air.

Over those first few months, as I walked my new neighborhood with my then best friend—an Irish setter pup I named after one of my favorite childhood movie characters, Shane—I began to realize that there was much more to Laurel Canyon than a bucolic place to hang one's hat. For one thing, virtually everyone's door was always open, literally and figuratively. Despite the grisly Manson murders just a year earlier in nearby Benedict Canyon—a tragedy that spread fear and paranoia throughout Los Angeles—this was still a veritable paradise. Strangers not only smiled at me and said hello—or flashed a peace sign—as we passed each other on the narrow streets, but sometimes they'd stop for a bit of conversation and even invite me into their homes for a bite to eat. Granted, it was a different, more trusting time—the era of love beads, bell-bottoms, and free-range hairstyles—but even back in the late '6os and early '70s, this extra level of friendliness was astonishing.

For another thing, there was almost always music drifting from the open windows of just about every house and cottage. And not just any old music, but thrilling new sounds, angelic harmonies and funky folksy riffs. When I started meeting and befriending the locals—people like Joni Mitchell, Linda Ronstadt, Carole King, David Crosby, and Stephen Stills, to name just a few of my immediate neighbors—it slowly began to dawn on me that I was not living in a normal residential zone. I had moved smack into the middle of a burgeoning musical renaissance.

A handful of the inhabitants were already celebrities. Micky Dolenz, who lived in a big house on Horse Shoe Canyon Road, and David Cassidy, who lived on Cole Crest Drive, both had hit TV shows in 1970—*The Monkees* and *The Partridge Family*. But many of the future musical superstars living in Laurel Canyon had not yet achieved the global fame that they would soon enjoy. Some, like Frank Zappa, another nearby neighbor, had already landed their first record deals. Others were still struggling to find their sound and make their rent. But, to me, all of them, famous or not, were merely the folks next door, my startlingly affable neighbors.

One thing almost everyone had in common in Laurel Canyon was that we were all transplants to the neighborhood: we had made a conscious choice to move here from a variety of far-flung origins. Zappa came from Baltimore. Mitchell was raised in Canada. Ronstadt hailed from Arizona. My own journey began in New York City. My dad, an immigrant from Poland, had worked his way up through the garment business and started his own company manufacturing plus-sized ladies' coats and suits. He made a decent enough living to afford a small but comfortable two-bedroom apartment—my younger sister and I shared one of them—in Washington Heights, which back in the 1950s was something of a starter neighborhood for Jewish families who were taking their first tentative steps into the middle class.

I was, to put it mildly, an unlikely candidate for a career in radio. For one thing, around the time I turned fifteen, I developed a severe stutter. Making my speech even more inelegant, I also had a strong New York accent. I was much smaller and slighter than most of my classmates, which, combined with my speech difficulties, put a bull's-eye on me for bullies, making me even more shy and awkward around strangers. The idea of speaking in front of others, even to small groups in classrooms, was terrifying. Indeed, as a teenager I had nightmares about it. I was also developing what would become lifelong insomnia, so sleep was increasingly rare.

Nevertheless, despite all those obstacles, the only thing in the world I wanted to be was a broadcaster.

I suppose it was precisely because of my adolescent isolation that I was drawn to radio and television. My only friends back then were on the airwaves. I spent countless hours as a kid listening to monologist Jean Shepherd spinning hypnotic spontaneous narratives on WOR Radio. When I was just a bit older, I became one-sided buddies with Jack Paar. I was watching NBC the night in 1960 when he famously walked off *The Tonight Show*; it traumatized me for days, as if I really had lost a best pal. Fortunately, my chum David Susskind remained on the air, hosting a local 11:00 p.m. television talk show called *Open End*. There was no stop time for the program: it kept going until the guests had run out of conversation. Perfect viewing for a budding young night owl.

One day, as I was getting ready to graduate high school, I told my father about my future career plans.

"Pop," I said, "I'm going into radio."

He sat back in his chair at the kitchen table and smiled.

"That's a good business," he replied in his Yiddish-tinged accent, patting my knee. "That appliance store on 181st Street—always busy. People always need to get those things fixed."

"Pop," I corrected him, "I'm not going to *repair* them; I'm going to be *inside* them. I'm going to be one of the people you hear on the radio. I'm going to be a broadcaster."

He looked at me as if I'd just told him I was joining the astronaut program.

I applied to nine different colleges with broadcasting departments and was accepted by only one: Los Angeles City College. So, in the summer of '63, I packed a bag, got on an airplane for the first time in my life, and turned up on its Hollywood campus with a stutter and a New York accent. And $300 for tuition.

They quickly put me through my paces, taught me how to look into a camera and make eye contact, how to do sportscasts and weather reports, and how to spin records and conduct interviews. (I enjoyed that last one the most.) Also, how to speak without a stutter or an accent.

The homework in this last area was a series of brutal but surprisingly effective breathing and talking exercises. I would come back from classes—I was leasing a tiny room between Sunset and Hollywood—lie down on the floor, put an eighteen-pound typewriter on my solar plexus, stick out my tongue, and say "Ahhhh" for as long as I could inhale and exhale. It didn't take too long before both my accent and stutter were beaten into submission.

I'd only been in school for about two or three months when I stumbled into the biggest break of my career, which, as it happened, occurred on one of the worst days in American history. We were attending classes on November 22, 1963, when the announcement came over the school speakers that President

Kennedy had been shot; students were instructed to go home. Most did, but a small group of us broadcasting kids headed to our department's bungalow and huddled around a black-and-white TV to watch Walter Cronkite's reportage of the assassination. A few hours into the newscast, the first photos of Lee Harvey Oswald started flashing onto the screen.

"That's Lee!" I heard one of my classmates exclaim. "I was in the Marines with that guy!"

I don't know how, during that horrible, tragic day, I had the presence of mind to recognize the massive opportunity that had just fallen into my lap. But I took my classmate—his name was Roland Bynum—into another room, sat down with him, and turned on my tape recorder. Honestly, it wasn't the most in-depth interview of my career—I was still very much a news radio novice—but it was definitely the most auspiciously timed. When I finished, I took the tape back to my one-room apartment and placed a call to the biggest local radio news station in L.A.

"Hi, my name is Elliot and I go to L.A. City College, and I just did an interview with a man who served in the Marine Corps with Lee Harvey Oswald," I told whoever answered the phone. "Would you like the tape?"

Within what seemed like a hundredth of a second, a courier turned up on a motorcycle to retrieve the recording. A few hundredths of a second later, my interview was being broadcast across the city. My phone started ringing off the hook, with outlets around the world reaching out. By the time the sun set that day, my little exclusive was airing nationally on the *CBS Evening News*.

I spent the next couple of years at L.A. City College honing my craft, becoming especially adept at the art of celebrity booking. I landed an interview with Jayne Mansfield—who back then was being presented by the studios as the new Marilyn Monroe— by pestering her agent with relentless letters and even acquiring a map to the stars' homes and writing one to Mansfield herself. She must have read my letter, because one day, while I was at home, warming up a bowl of split pea soup on my hot plate, my phone rang. I was astonished to hear her voice on the other end. She not only agreed to the interview but invited me to a party at her house in Beverly Hills. Not long after that, I spotted Sal Mineo at a bar in Hollywood where I'd gone to cover a stage hypnotist. I landed an interview with the *Rebel Without a Cause* actor as well. In fact, Sal and I ended up becoming close friends.

After I graduated from City College, I set out to look for my first real job in radio. I found one at a listener supported station called KPFK, which on the face of it didn't necessarily seem like a perfect fit for me. Back then, listener-supported radio appealed mostly to older people, so KPFK played a lot of harpsichord music. Sometimes it would broadcast lectures on bird-watching. But I had a plan for the station, which I pitched during my job interview.

"Look," I said, "I know I'm only a kid and I just got out of school, but I have an idea for a telephone talk show for teenagers. I want to interview people that teens are interested in, like rock stars. I could do it three nights a week, from ten p.m. to two a.m. We'd call it *Looking in with Elliot Mintz.*"

The station manager gave me the same skeptical look my father had in our kitchen but for some reason said yes—and that's how, at twenty-one, I became the youngest radio talk show host in America.

I focused my interviews at KPFK on the musicians and artists that nobody else would book, which in those days was pretty much everyone in the counterculture. Remember, this was when the three broadcast networks—ABC, NBC, and CBS—had a stranglehold on the airwaves. Nobody was interviewing rock stars and beat poets, not on radio and certainly not on TV. Johnny Carson was never going to invite Frank Zappa or Allen Ginsberg as guests. For a while, I was the only game in town.

It was, I have to admit, a pretty cushy gig, especially for an insomniac. Since my show was a late-night program, I would get home from work at around 3:00 a.m., smoke a joint, read a book, relax, go to bed, and sleep till noon. Then I'd drift into the station in the afternoon and plan my night's programming. For this not-so-grueling labor, I was paid the handsome sum of $65 a week, just enough to afford my first car, a used 1964 Morris Minor, for which I paid $300. Best of all, my show rapidly began attracting an audience, which wasn't all that surprising given the youthquake rumbling across the country at the time. I was hardly becoming famous—fame was never my goal anyway—but I was getting noticed within the broadcasting community.

In fact, before long, I was approached by a bigger commercial radio station, KLAC, which offered me much better money—$300 a week—for essentially the same job, being the host of a talk show aimed at young listeners. And so it went for the next few years as I climbed L.A.'s radio station food chain, landing different jobs, sometimes stumbling and losing them, but always ultimately finding another, until I eventually ended up on KLOS, the station where, in the fall of 1971, I would conduct what would turn out to be the most consequential interview of my life.

Although I was primarily a talk show host and not a DJ, part of my job was to stay abreast of the latest music releases so I could keep my guest list fresh and interesting. A lot of the people I interviewed on my shows were friends. One of the advantages of moving to that little house with the hillevator in Laurel Canyon was that the neighborhood provided an endless source of potential interviewees; I could book a guest just by walking my dog around the block and seeing who I'd bump into. But I also spent many hours sitting at home by my turntable with stacks of new vinyl releases—the record companies sent me twenty to thirty every week—listening for a voice that pricked up my ears.

On that day in September 1971, I found one.

I knew, of course, who Yoko Ono was; everybody did. She was John Lennon's wife, a somewhat divisive figure back then—and still today—who many people blamed (unfairly) for busting up the Beatles.

Full disclosure: I was never a Beatles superfan. I obviously appreciated their music, understood their staggering genius, and acknowledged their enormous contribution to pop culture. But I was raised on Elvis. Presley was king during my formative teen years, so I felt more connected to "Jailhouse Rock" than "I Want to Hold Your Hand." Indeed, by the time *With the Beatles* arrived in America, I had already left home and was studying at City College. (In fact, in what may have been the worst-timed releases in music industry history, the album dropped the same day Kennedy was shot.)

Still, I'd admired John and Yoko as cultural figures even before the Beatles broke up in 1970. I had followed the extensive reporting of their "bed-ins for peace" in 1969, when the two of them, just after getting married, camped out in their pajamas in hotel rooms in Amsterdam and Montreal and held free-form discussions with members of the world press about ending the then raging war in Vietnam. Aside from being incredibly brave politically—John and Yoko both had spots of honor on Nixon's enemies list and were regularly surveilled by the FBI—I respected their inspired public relations sleight of hand. They got the press to carry their message—in this case, the senselessness of the bloodshed in Southeast Asia—by inviting them to their honeymoon. Brilliant.

But on this portentous fall afternoon, as I plucked Yoko's *Fly* from the stacks of new releases I'd just received from the record companies, I gave her another look. How could I not? Filling the album's front cover was an arresting close-up photograph of Yoko's face, a distorted double-exposed Polaroid shot through curved glass that made it look like she was crying. The photographer, I saw in the notes, was John.

If the cover made me curious, I was full-on fascinated when I put the record on my turntable. I'd never heard anything like it in my life. It was conceptual and experimental, confusing and elusive, but also somehow inspiring. There was raw visceral pain in Yoko's voice, a completely different sound than the sweet harmonies drifting through the open windows of my neighborhood. It was a double album, thirteen tracks, ninety-four minutes, but I listened to it twice. When I was done, I knew two things. First, I wanted to play the record on the radio. And second, I wanted to speak to the person who made it.

Back in the '70s, booking a radio guest was a relatively simple if sometimes grueling endeavor. All you had to do was place twenty or thirty phone calls. That was the disadvantage of wrangling talent in pre-internet, pre-email days: it required an enormous amount of dialing. You'd need to contact the record label (usually in New York) to find the name of the publicist handling the artist, then call that publicist to make the request, then the publicist would have to try to track down the artist or the artist's manager and call them before calling you back.

Landing Yoko for my radio show, though, couldn't have been quicker or easier. I called the record label, told them I wanted to play the album on the air and interview its creator over the phone during my broadcast. A day later, I was talking to Yoko's assistant.

"How's Sunday night?" he said.

I like to be prepared for my interviews, so I usually do a bit of research. In Yoko's case, I started by rereading *Grapefruit*, the conceptual literary artwork she published in 1964, two years before she met John Lennon. People tend to forget that Yoko was an accomplished artist in her own right, with her own storied background. The daughter of a powerful banker in Japan, she went to middle school with future emperor Prince Akihito, studied at Sarah Lawrence in New York, then fell in with a downtown avant-garde scene in Manhattan.

After launching her own art career—with performances like her famous 1964 interactive work *Cut Piece*, during which she sat passively while audience members were given scissors and invited to sheer off parts of the dress she was wearing—she moved to London with her husband at the time, filmmaker Anthony Cox. She met John at an art gallery that was exhibiting her works and divorced Cox a couple years later. (John divorced his first wife, Cynthia Lennon, around the same time.)

Grapefruit was one of Yoko's more accessible and whimsical artistic works. It was a simple, square-shaped "Book of Instructions," one on each page, written not quite in haiku but something sort of like it, giving readers minor mental exercises to perform. "Imagine the clouds dripping. Dig a hole in your garden to put them in," read one. Another: "Imagine one thousand suns in the sky at the same time. Let them shine for one hour. Then, let them gradually melt into the sky. Make one tuna fish sandwich and eat."

Although I confess I did not follow all the instructions, it was unlike anything I'd ever read before.

Setting up the interview, I can't say my expectations were high. It didn't feel like my interview with Yoko was going to be a giant one. I didn't get the feeling that people were going to be talking about it after it aired the way they did when I interviewed Jack Nicholson or Groucho Marx. Hers at that time was not a voice people were clamoring to hear. Still, I was intrigued by her art and her reputation, and I was looking forward to what I assumed would be a onetime interview.

Yoko's assistant had given me a private phone number to call on Sunday night at 9:00 p.m. Pacific time. She was in New York, so it would be midnight for her. I arrived at my radio booth at KLOS at around 8:45, nodded hello to my producer, Barney, who sat behind a wall of glass, and went about my usual preparations. I turned down the lights, lit a candle and a stick of incense, adjusted my microphone, and, just after the clock struck nine, started dialing Yoko's phone number. I had absolutely no idea how my life was about to change.

The phone rang only twice before she picked up.

"Hello!" she said. "This is Yoko."

TWO

Los Angeles, 1971

Before it snows, dogs start to get happy. They start to wag their tails."

"I didn't know that," I responded.

"Oh, I didn't know that, either, but somebody told me about it. I don't even know if it's true or not. But then, I'm not a dog."

Our interview went on like this for some forty minutes, a swirling murmuration of thoughts and ideas—sometimes connected, oftentimes not—as I explored for the first time, on live radio, the thronging aviary that was Yoko Ono's mind.

We talked about music and art ("It doesn't involve talent to become an artist; it only involves a certain frame of mind"). We talked about dreams ("Most of my dreams are connected with something to do with color"). We talked about politics and peace and her vision of utopia ("I believe in total freedom and the world of total freedom would come when there is total communication").

Practically the only thing we didn't talk about, at least not directly, was her relationship with John. This was a deliberate choice—I knew Yoko had been grilled about her husband in virtually every interview she'd given since they met in 1966, so I decided not to go there. I wanted our conversation to be different, to focus entirely on her and her work.

Still, inevitably, John came up. In fact, in retrospect, the most poignant—and chilling—exchange of that first interview came when I asked Yoko, who was then thirty-eight years old, if she ever thought about death. "Oh, yes, sometimes we do," she said, answering for the both of them. "The thing that worries us the most is which one will die first, because that's one thing we can't control. John and I talk about it a lot. John couldn't stand that I would go first, so he would always say, 'You have to let me go first.' These days, he's started to realize how vulnerable I am, and he's concerned about me more. Sometimes he says, 'Well, I can't go first, because I can't leave you alone.'"

"Do you take precautions?" I asked.

"No, I'm afraid we're not very careful. But we're concerned about each other's health. We try to stop each other from smoking excessively. But other than that, we're not very careful."

"And when you're gone, how would you like to be remembered?" I asked her.

"John and I lived, loved, and died," she answered.

Even this early in my career, I'd already interviewed hundreds of musicians and artists. Many of them were inspiring, others not so much. Let's just say some artists speak more eloquently through their work than they do on the radio. As for this interview with Yoko, I felt it went well: judging from the phone calls afterwards, listeners seemed to enjoy it. From my point of view, Yoko was interesting and engaging, but, to be honest, it didn't stand out to me as one of my more groundbreaking broadcasting moments.

Still, there was *something* about our conversation that lingered in my mind. At two in the morning, after I signed off the air, I drove back to Laurel Canyon in my old Morris Minor and tried to put a finger on it. As I wheeled my way along Sunset, I began to realize that it wasn't anything Yoko had said that was sticking in my head but how she made me *feel*. Which was oddly comfortable and familiar, as if we'd known each other for ages and were simply continuing a conversation we'd been having for years. That's not something I'd often felt with a stranger, certainly not on the air during an interview.

But by the time I'd parked at Oak Court, ridden the hillevator to my door, and settled in for my after-work routine, I'd moved onto other thoughts.

I know most people look upon insomnia as an affliction, something to battle and overcome. I used to view it that way, but not any longer. Although I've occasionally endeavored to tinker with my sleep schedule—I once spent a night at the Stanford research lab with wires hooked into practically every inch of my body, analyzing my resting rhythms, only to have the doctor announce in the morning that I had insomnia ("That'll be $2,000, please")—I had more or less come to peace with my nocturnal nature.

Indeed, I'd grown to appreciate the late-night hours, the way the city lights twinkled in the distance down the hill, the sounds of crickets and owls, the velvety solitude of the dark. After my shift at the radio station, there was nothing more calming than curling up with a good book on my sofa, firing up a poorly rolled joint—I never did get the hang of that—and blissing out in my Laurel Canyon hideaway.

Of course, it was also the 1970s, I was in my twenties and living in L.A.—then the free love capital of the Western world—so I didn't spend all my nights at home.

There wasn't much action in Laurel Canyon—no nightclubs, restaurants, or movie theaters, nothing of a commercial nature, just people making music, making love, and smoking pot. So if you wanted nightlife—and I certainly did—you'd have to drive a mile and a half down the hill, where you'd find the Troubadour, the Roxy, and Whisky a Go Go. (I was at Whisky a Go Go the first time the Doors played there; when I saw Jim Morrison come out onstage, I thought to myself, *If James Dean had decided to sing instead of act . . .*)

The Sunset Strip and the scene there was a major part of my life. Many of my off-air evenings were whiled away at Dan Tana's, just down the road; there were always old friends—and potential new ones—eating and drinking at that fabled West Hollywood bistro. And there was the Troubadour, the famed rock 'n' roll club, where I spent many of my recreational evenings watching live performances by the likes of Cat Stevens, Van Morrison, and Don Henley, to name a few legendary acts. As a local radio "personality" and increasingly "well-known" rock interviewer, I was extended some special courtesies by the club: let's just say I never had to wait in line at the door. And while I was never what one might describe as a female magnet, in those days it wasn't particularly difficult to find companionship, even if you weren't a rock star.

In any case, the day after the Yoko interview, I woke up at my usual hour—the crack of noon—and began my not-so-vigorous daily rituals. I brewed myself a cup of herbal tea, did some light exercising and a little meditation. Then I took Shane for a long walk around Laurel Canyon. When I got back, I sifted through my mail, scanned the newspaper headlines, and started thinking about my show for that evening: I needed to call my producer, Barney, and run through our guest options. I was brewing my second cup of tea when the phone rang.

"Hello, Elliot, this is Yoko," she said, without pausing for a response. "I was very happy with the interview we did last night. I liked the questions you asked. You gave me the space to express myself."

I opened my mouth to say something, but she kept speaking.

"I've done interviews with John—he and I together—but I

never get a chance to speak," she said. "The interviewers really want to talk to John, not to me, so they don't ask me any questions. I've begun to develop a stutter because of it. I feel as if I have to rush into the conversation if I want to say something before the interviewer interrupts me and talks to John. It's made me inhibited in my speaking."

She paused for a breath. "Sometimes," she continued, "it's very difficult being me."

Now, keep in mind, I had just picked up the phone and said hello—that was it. I hadn't uttered another word. Yoko just rolled straight into a conversation as if we really had been friends for years. This, I would quickly learn, was the energy signature that would come to define our entire relationship. At the moment, though, I was so startled by her call, all I could do was try to keep up and process what she was saying.

"I imagine it would be very difficult being you," I finally managed to blurt out.

"You know, sometimes when they come for an interview, they'll ask us to go into separate rooms, John in one and me in the other," she went on. "They'll say they're going to interview each of us and then put the two interviews together for the radio or the newspaper. But they're in the room with John for an hour and a half and they talk to me for maybe ten minutes. And then, when I read the article later, I'm not in it at all."

"Does that hurt your feelings?" I asked, not knowing what else to say.

"Well, it always hurts my feelings, you know," she said. "But the best way to handle hurt feelings is to feel better. So I remove those people from my mind."

"That must make it hard for you to do interviews, knowing that the interviewers are always going to be asking you about John."

"No, because I always hope the next person who asks me questions will give me a chance to talk."

We chatted like this for about forty minutes, maybe longer, and then, without warning, Yoko announced, "I have to go," and hung up.

I was, to put it mildly, flabbergasted.

It wasn't that someone famous had phoned me out of the blue at my home. I was never in the least bit starstruck. I'd interviewed enough celebrities by that point to be immune to fame's charms. No, what had me reeling was the sheer magnanimity of the gesture. Nobody I had ever interviewed before—or, for that matter, since—had ever bothered to call to say thank you. It was a simple thing, but it was so shockingly thoughtful and unexpected, it blew me away.

And then, even more surprising, she called again the very next day.

This time, it was five in the morning, an awkward hour even for an insomniac, although slightly less so for her, in New York, where it was a somewhat more respectable 8:00 a.m. But I was pleased to hear from her again, even if I was only half conscious.

I struggled to shake the sleep from my brain as she launched right back into our conversation from the day before.

"So anyway, I've just finished reading a book," she said, without so much as a hello. "It's a mystery because I like mysteries. I mostly read mysteries."

I later realized that this was the way Yoko started every conversation—each one seemed to be an unbroken extension of our last one. There was no need for pleasantries or apologies. It was a never-ending loop.

That day, I was groggy but was able to cough out a response. "Um, that's surprising," I said. "I would think you'd read a lot about art, being an artist."

"Artists don't read about art," she said. "Artists just create art."

"What is it about mysteries that fascinate you?"

"Well, you don't know the ending unless you're very smart and can figure it out."

"Is it important to you to figure out the whodunit part?"

"It's important for me to see how the author makes the mystery invisible to the reader, how he or she makes it difficult for the reader to guess the ending."

"I'm curious what else you're reading besides mysteries," I said.

"Why?" she asked.

"I just thought there might be other books that interest you."

"I read three or four books at a time," she said. "There are always books around me. Same with John. We start and stop with different books and sometimes we exchange them. Right now, I'm also reading a book about vegetarianism because I'm thinking of changing my diet."

"So," I said, still shaking the sleep from my head, "you're currently reading a book about vegetarianism and you're also in the middle of a mystery novel—"

"Elliot," she interrupted, sounding irritated. "I just told you that I *finished* reading a mystery, remember?"

I was learning lesson number one when talking to Yoko: Pay attention.

The second call went on longer than the first—maybe ninety minutes. I remember seeing the sun coming up as we spoke. Much of the conversation was filled with the sort of cozy chit-chat old friends engage in when there isn't anything important to discuss. Still, it was revealing in its own way.

"What do you eat when you wake up?" she asked me at one point.

"I like fresh fruit and some tea," I said.

"Do you put sweetener in your tea?"

"Yes, I do. I like sweetener in my tea."

"You shouldn't do that," she said. "You can't stay healthy with artificial things."

"Well, what do you eat in the morning?" I asked.

"I don't eat when I wake up," she answered. "I take an ice bath. Every morning the assistants fill the bathtub with ice cubes and turn on the cold water, and I get into the tub and stay very still. That's how I start my day."

"Why would you do that?" I asked, horrified. My preferred method of waking was a long, slow, gentle glide path to consciousness. An ice bath first thing in the morning sounded like a nightmare.

"It's very good for the circulation," she said. "It's very important for the way the blood moves through the body. The blood stops at the heart, where it gets inspiration. It flows to the brain, where it gets knowledge. It flows to different parts of the body to give you balance and strength . . ."

It was, I had to admit, a beautiful dissertation on the virtues of ice baths. But I still didn't want to take one.

As with her first call, the second ended abruptly and unceremoniously with Yoko announcing that she had to go. Before she left, though, she gave me a number where I could reach her—an even more private line than the one her assistant had shared with me for the radio interview—and invited me to call her whenever I wanted. Which I did, the very next day, for reasons I'm not certain I can explain.

I suppose part of it was good manners. She had called me twice; didn't I now owe her a call? Part of it may have also been curiosity, just to see where this new phone friendship might ultimately lead. Whatever the reason, this third call—fourth, if you include the radio interview—was a continuation of our previous exchanges. Indeed, as I would discover over the coming decades, all my phone calls with Yoko, no matter how far spaced apart, were all a continuation of the same single epically long conversation.

"I tried the tea without sweetener," I told her. "And I didn't like it. What about honey? Can I put honey in my tea?"

"Elliot," she said, "that's the way tea is supposed to taste. Why would you put something in it to make it taste differently? You should eat and taste food the way food is meant to be eaten and tasted. You shouldn't have to add anything to it, because there is nothing missing from the food."

"But what about honey?" I repeated. "Honey is natural."

"Elliot, didn't I just explain it to you? Were you not paying attention?"

As it happens, my polite return call to Yoko wasn't really necessary; she would continue over the coming weeks and months—and years—to phone me just about every day, at all hours, with no warning. Sometimes it was to discuss a dream she'd had, other times to talk about an artist she'd just met. Occasionally she would call because she'd written a new song and wanted to sing it for me over the phone.

At first, I was delighted that she found me a worthwhile conversational companion. And the calls themselves were somehow always fascinating to me. Yoko had a unique way of thinking that made me see the world just a little bit differently, even when talking about subjects as simple as tea sweeteners.

But, of course, I also knew that these phone calls were unusual, even odd. Why would Yoko Ono, of all people, suddenly take such an intense interest in a twenty-six-year-old radio host in L.A.? It didn't make a lot of sense at the time. All these years later, it's still difficult to comprehend. I've been asked a million times what Yoko saw in me back then—why out of all the humans on the planet, she chose to befriend Elliot Mintz. The honest answer is: I have no idea. You'd have to ask her.

All I do know is that at a certain point, as the calls continued to ramp up through the fall of 1971, I began to get the disorienting sense that my life was taking a turn into uncharted territory. My budding relationship with Yoko was unlike any I'd ever entered into before: she was, in a way, becoming something like a teacher to me, a sage and learned guide, and I her young disciple—but it was reshaping my world in ways that could occasionally feel quite awkward.

For instance, shortly after Yoko started calling, I was at home in Laurel Canyon with a young lady. We first encountered each other earlier that evening at the Troubadour, where I'd gone to see Kris Kristofferson perform. I'm ashamed to admit I no longer remember her name—let's call her, in the spirit of the '70s, Luna—but I vividly recall how stunningly beautiful she was, with long dark hair and a flawless olive complexion. We got to talking, and drinking, and smoking, and before we knew it, we were closing the club. Next thing we knew, we were riding the hillevator up to my door; I believe that might have been where we first kissed. Once inside my house, I asked if she wanted another drink, but she was already heading upstairs to my bedroom.

Flash-forward a few hours and Luna was asleep in my bed, our clothes strewn over the floor. It was something like four in the morning and I wasn't quite ready to fall asleep. Instead, I lay in bed next to her and admired the soft curve of her hip barely covered by the edge of my sheets, letting myself ponder if perhaps I'd found my forever-elusive soul mate.

Then the phone rang.

I dashed downstairs to pick it up before the ringing would wake Luna. A more chivalrous man might have unplugged the phone or ignored the call. In hindsight, maybe that's what I should have done. But I knew who was on the other end of the line and I felt compelled to answer it.

"I'm going on a diet," Yoko announced. Again, no hello, no pleasantries, just an abrupt continuation of the never-ending conversation.

"Why?" I asked. "I see lots of pictures of you in the newspapers and I've seen you on television. You don't look like you have a weight problem."

"I'm going to do a photo shoot and I need to lose weight. What's the best way to do that? You live in Hollywood. How do people there lose weight?"

At the time, there was a famous Dr. Feelgood type in L.A. who'd been injecting movie stars with a weight-loss elixir—it was called human chorionic gonadotropin, or hCG—primarily consisting of pregnant women's urine. I knew from my own limited personal experience that this magic potion was indeed able to melt away fat. Despite Yoko's warnings about the evils of artificial sweeteners, she seemed keen to learn more.

"Can you get me some?" she asked.

After I explained how only a doctor could provide a patient

with the injections, our conversation veered into other matters. We talked for about ninety minutes, until Yoko hung up. When I groggily climbed back upstairs, I saw Luna sitting up in my bed, wide-awake.

"Who was that?" she softly inquired. "Is everything okay?"

I could see in Luna's eyes what she was thinking. *Was this guy married? Did he have a girlfriend?*

"Everything's fine," I said. "It was just a friend. Nothing important."

"But you were on the phone for over an hour," she persisted.

I hemmed and hawed. "I have a special friend in New York, and we talk late at night," I offered weakly, which only made Luna more confused. "There's really nothing to worry about," I added. "It was nothing."

The phone call, and my clumsy evasiveness about it, had clearly thrown a wet blanket on what had otherwise been a lovely encounter. Luna kept asking about it, I kept equivocating, and before long my presumed soul mate was gathering her clothes from the floor and preparing to leave.

I thought about coming clean with Luna. I thought about telling her that it was Yoko Ono on the phone. But it somehow felt wrong, as if I'd be violating some unspoken code of trust. Plus, even if I had told the truth, I suspected it would have only made things worse, certainly more complicated. I could imagine Luna's reaction: *Why is this nice guy I just slept with talking on the phone at four in the morning with John Lennon's wife, the woman who broke up the Beatles?*

If I couldn't fully explain to myself why I had just spent ninety minutes on the phone with Yoko, how could I expect Luna to understand it?

So I kept quiet as she slipped into her boots, grabbed her bag, and marched downstairs to call a cab. That's when it started to dawn on me how much this strange new phone friendship was going to impact my life.

And Yoko was just the beginning.

I was about to meet John.

THREE

Los Angeles, 1971

I f you've ever heard John Lennon talk—and who at this point hasn't?—you know he spoke like nobody else.

There was something about the way he put sentences together—a wholly distinct cadence, a gleeful inventiveness with the language, a unique vocal playfulness—that was all his own and that has always been impossible to replicate in written words. I've devoured countless tomes about John, pored over hundreds of interviews with him, and nowhere have I ever encountered a printed quote that accurately captured what he sounded like in real life.

Attempting to reproduce John's voice in the pages of a book, even this one, is like trying to put vapor on paper. It simply can't be done.

That said, I am reasonably confident I can correctly portray

the *content* of my many conversations with John over the years—
I can convey his words if not the actual *sounds* of his words—
starting with our very first talk on my radio show on the night
of October 9, 1971, his thirty-first birthday.

Yoko—whose voice, incidentally, is considerably easier to
transfer onto paper—was the one who arranged the interview. In
fact, she's the one who, several weeks after we'd started our now
almost daily telephone calls, suggested I talk to John in the first
place.

We'd been on the phone discussing, of all things, J. Krishnamurti, the Indian philosopher whose latest book I was in the
middle of reading. "I read a lot of metaphysical stuff," I told her.
"And he's got a new book out with excerpts from some of his
lectures."

"*Freedom from the Known,*" she said.

I was impressed. Although Krishnamurti was widely read
within a certain spiritually minded milieu in the 1970s, his books
weren't exactly massive bestsellers. "John's reading it, too," she
added.

"Is he a fan of Krishnamurti?" I asked.

"No," she answered. "He wouldn't call himself a fan. John
doesn't like the word 'fan.' He just seems to be responding well
to this particular guy."

"You should read it, too," I suggested.

"No," she said. "I don't read those sorts of books."

"You might like it," I pressed on. "Maybe you should talk to
John about it."

"Maybe *you* should talk to him about it," she said.

Now, it wasn't like I had been fishing for this invitation. John was not a subject Yoko and I spoke much about in the first months of our telephonic friendship. I never asked Yoko direct questions about her husband, never expressed more than polite, friendly interest in his comings and goings. The focus in those early days was entirely on her—both because she was genuinely the one who I wanted to speak to, but also because I knew how many people had seen Yoko as simply the gateway to John, and I was determined not to join that number. But, of course, I was keenly aware that the man she was married to—who might very well be napping in the room next door during our increasingly lengthy late-night phone chats—was a philosophical thinker of some note himself.

Also, to be honest, I was curious what John thought about his wife spending so much time on the phone with another man.

"Does John ever have an issue with you talking to me?" I asked Yoko.

"Of course not. Why would you think so?"

"Because most husbands would have some degree of concern or suspicion if their wives spent hours talking to another man on the phone in the middle of the night."

"You're inflating your ego, aren't you, Elliot?"

"I'm just being curious," I said.

"You're just being negative," she responded.

"Well," I said, awkwardly changing gears, "I would love to talk to John any time he wants."

"It's John's birthday on October 9," she said. "Maybe you can speak with him then. On your radio show."

"John doesn't have anything else he'd rather do on his birthday?" I asked, surprised by the proposition.

"He doesn't care about his birthdays," Yoko said.

JOHN had just released *Imagine* a month earlier and had already done quite a bit of publicity for the album, including his now iconic appearance with Yoko on *The Dick Cavett Show*, during which the couple chain-smoked cigarettes and good-naturedly pushed back against the rumors that Yoko had "busted up" the Beatles. I paid a lot of attention to John and Yoko's interviews in those early days—even before we started talking on the phone—as well as to the people interviewing them. Part of it was professional curiosity; after all, talking to artists was now my livelihood, too. But it was also that John and Yoko could be terrifically entertaining interviewees. Even a famously erudite host like Cavett had a hard time keeping up with their razor-sharp banter.

This time I didn't bother doing any research before the interview. I didn't need to. Like most conscious beings on planet Earth in 1971, I already knew a lot about his origin story. How he had been raised by his aunt Mimi in postwar Liverpool, how his mother had died in a tragic accident (struck by a car driven by an off-duty policeman), how as a teenager he had met Paul McCartney at a church fete—to anyone with a passing knowledge of pop music history, it was all basic Beatles lore. Plus, because of my friendship with Yoko, I felt I might have more insight into the man than most interviewers. Maybe even more than Cavett.

A few days later, I was sitting in my DJ booth, dialing the phone. I admit I felt a bit more nervous than I had before calling Yoko for the first time. I always had in the back of my mind a sense of who the biggest gets were in radio—and a former Beatle was among the biggest of the big. But I'd been talking to Yoko for weeks, and certainly gained a sense of John through our conversations. Leading up to my interview with John, which was live on the air, I didn't know what was going to happen. I'd heard other interviews and knew he had his moods, had his feelings. And I was concerned about the language issues as well—if he'd use a four-letter word on live radio. I was worried it was going to be unruly.

"Yeah, hello?" John said after it rang twice. He sounded normal, calm.

Since he'd just turned thirty-one, I started the interview by asking him about getting older.

"Me auntie Mimi used to always say to me that thirty is the right age for a man and I thought she was giving me a lot of bull, you know," he answered. "But in a way she was right. It's a good age because you're not old but you've sort of had some experience."

I asked him if he'd had any regrets about anything during his first thirty years of life.

"I think I'm the happiest I've ever been. I have Yoko, and

that's all that really matters to me. And I feel as though if I'd been or done anything else, I would not have met her."

I asked him about living in New York as opposed to London—whether the pace was different.

"Oh, no," he said. "Because Yoko and I always live at about two thousand light-years' speed when we're working, or there's just absolutely no movement at all. It's one extreme or the other, but it's usually moving very fast and there's always a small hurricane around us."

The interview went on for some forty minutes. At one point there was a harrowing technical glitch: about seven minutes in, the call got dropped, every radio host's nightmare. Fortunately, it was reconnected after a few frantic seconds. And there were one or two other rough patches, like at the end, when I said goodbye to John—the man who'd just released a song imploring listeners to imagine a world with no religion—by saying to him, "God bless." But for the most part I was quite pleased with how our conversation turned out. Afterward, driving to Laurel Canyon at 2:00 a.m., I wondered how many people had tuned in. I hoped at least a few.

Turned out, a lot had.

The day after the interview, I took Shane for a stroll. There were the usual waves and smiles as I passed acquaintances on the dirt roads and paths that made up the labyrinth of the neighborhood. But, to my surprise, more than a few of them stopped me to comment about how much they enjoyed the Lennon interview, remarking on how comfortable John seemed with me.

Later, when I drove to Sunset Boulevard for a haircut, I was seated in a chair between two patrons who were deeply engaged in conversation. As my barber snipped at my shoulder-length '70s locks, I began to realize they were talking about the radio chat with John. Obviously, they had no idea the shaggy-haired customer sitting between them was the host of that interview. (This sort of moment, by the way, was one of the great perks of being a radio host: since so few of my listeners knew what I looked like, I could listen in on people's conversations about me without anybody being the wiser.)

A little later that day, back at home, my phone rang, and for once it wasn't Yoko. "Hey, Elliot, what are you doing?" David Cassidy asked me. "Can I come over?"

David and I had become friendly, one of the many casual hanging-out pals I'd made in Laurel Canyon. He was five years younger than me but at the time was at the height of his TV fame. Hordes of fans, mostly teenage girls, would swarm outside his house on Cole Crest Drive, hoping to catch a glimpse of the dreamy Keith Partridge. Whenever he popped over to my place, David would avoid the throng by ducking out his backyard and following a "secret" path through a wooded plot of land that abutted his house and mine.

"I loved your interview with Lennon," he told me, lounging on my Naugahyde sofa as I uncorked a bottle of wine. David, like a lot of my musician friends in Laurel Canyon, was obsessed with John, so I took this as a high compliment.

"I'm so glad you liked it," I said.

"You're so lucky," he went on. "I'd give *anything* to meet him."

As I poured each of us a glass, I fleetingly considered telling David about my phone calls with Yoko. It was tempting. I knew he would find the revelation that I was in regular contact with the woman who shared his idol's life fascinating. But just as I had with Luna, I bit my tongue. Although it hadn't yet been stated out loud, I instinctively understood that my phone relationship with Yoko was a delicate affair. If I started blabbing, it would shatter our trust. And I wanted that trust to grow and go both ways: Yoko had shared so much with me, and I'd shared a great deal about myself in return. I decided that, for the time being at least, I would keep the calls to myself.

In the days that followed, as more and more friends (and strangers) complimented me on the show—dropping by my table at Dan Tana's to offer kudos, shouting in my ear about it while I was listening to a set at the Troubadour—I considered phoning John to thank him for the interview. I wondered if he might be expecting a call, since he knew I was now such close pals with his wife. Wouldn't it be the polite thing to do? Wasn't it common courtesy?

Ultimately, though, I decided against it. I was grateful John had granted me forty minutes for the radio interview. I was thankful it had gone over so well with the public. But I didn't want to intrude on his life any more than I already had.

But then, maybe about a week later, as I was climbing into bed at my usual hour—around four in the morning—John called me.

"Is that Elliot?" I heard a slightly nasal voice with a Liverpool accent say on the other end of the line. "John here. How are you?"

I was quite groggy and more than a little surprised, so without thinking I blurted out, "I'm just going to bed."

He laughed. "At this hour?" It was seven in the morning on the East Coast, so he must have just woken up. But he must have also been aware of the time in L.A. Or maybe not? Either way, he went on, "Can you talk for a few minutes?"

That focused my attention: John Lennon was asking *me* if I had the time to speak with *him*. What might he say? John was so well-known for his thoughtful and philosophical songs and lyrics, who knew what sort of soaring, inspiring conversation might be in store for me, what magnificent revelations he was about to bestow upon me. I was totally unprepared for what actually came next.

"I talked to Mother," he said—Mother, of course, was the way he always referred to Yoko. "She told me about these weight-loss pills you took."

"Weight-loss injections," I corrected him, already surprised by the question and slightly taken aback.

"Do you have a weight problem?" he asked.

I didn't. I told him that I had put on a few pounds at one point and tried the then somewhat rare hCG injections. But at that moment, two other thoughts were racing through my mind besides explaining to John that I wasn't overweight. The first was that neither John nor Yoko had the slightest idea what I looked like. I, of course, had seen thousands of images of them. But from their point of view my physical being was a complete mystery. I was just a disembodied, somewhat monotone voice on the phone. The second thought was that Yoko had obviously been sharing details of our conversations with her husband. What else had she told him about me?

"Can you get me some?" John asked. "Can you get me some of them pills?"

"John," I said, "there seems to be some confusion here. They aren't pills—they're injections that a doctor gives you."

"Injections?" he repeated.

"Yes, with a syringe," I said.

"In your arse or your arm?" he asked.

"Um, I got mine in my rear end."

There was a brief pause. I could all but hear John thinking.

"Are you sure they don't come in pill form?" he asked.

"I'm pretty sure," I said.

"Is it something I can inject meself?"

"I don't think so. It would mean you'd need a needle and the drug, and you'd have to know precisely how much to administer. I don't think any doctor would let you do that on your own."

For the next few minutes, John went on a semi-rage against the medical establishment. "They don't want you to have it in a bloody pill so that you have to go to daddy doctor to get it," he fumed. "But there's nothing daddy doctors can do fer you that you can't do fer yourself."

"What about open-heart surgery?" I kidded. "You can't do that by yourself."

He laughed. "How do you know? Have you ever tried?

"Look, Elliot," he went on, his voice suddenly more serious, "I'm just looking to appear fit. Can you call around and see if you can get me the injections? Would you do that for me?"

As I was to learn later, John and Yoko were obsessed with weight. John had struggled his whole life with it. He used to joke that back when they filmed *Help!* he was in his "fat Elvis" period: he was very self-conscious about that and took it very seriously. He'd tried every fad diet in the world and was clearly open to any other new weight-loss methods that came along. When the call ended after about thirty minutes, I slipped back into bed, pulled the covers over my head, and again thought about what had just happened. John had called me at four in the morning not to thank me for the interview, as Yoko had done, or further engage in some finer point of our radio conversation. No, he had called because he wanted me to procure fat-melting injections for him—or, better still, fat-melting pills. Yoko was equally fixated with her weight. They even organized their gigantic walk-in closet—actually, more of a walk-in room the size of a small boutique—according to their fluctuating sizes, with department store–style clothing carousels numbered by their waist measurements.

At the time, though, receiving a phone call from John Lennon asking me for help in obtaining diet pills struck me as supremely bizarre.

And yet, just as bizarrely, I found myself complying. First thing in the morning—well, around noonish—I called my doctor. Naturally, the nurse told me there was no way to get the injections and confirmed that it most certainly did not come in pill form. I thanked her and hung up. Then I called an acquaintance with certain gray market pharmacological connections. He also told me it was impossible to get without going to the doctor.

I called John.

"Look," I said, "I really hate to disappoint you but—"

"You can't get it fer me," he finished my sentence.

"No, but maybe I can find somebody in New York who can give you the injections."

"You mean a daddy doctor that I would have to go to?"

"Yes," I said. "I understand that would pose certain logistical problems for you, but there's no other way unless we can find a doctor who would come to you."

He seemed disappointed but didn't linger on it too long. In fact, his next question took me completely by surprise. "Are you from Canada?" he asked. "Because you sound Canadian."

I laughed and told him about my stuttering problem as a teenager—how I'd been trained out of it, as well as my New York accent, when I studied broadcasting at City College, and how it resulted in a neutral speaking style that apparently to him sounded Canadian. After ten or fifteen minutes of more pleasantries, John just hung up the phone. Like his wife, he rarely said goodbye.

The next day Yoko phoned, which, of course, was not at all

surprising, since she was calling at least once a day, a pattern that I still found delightful if somewhat perplexing. What was different this time, however, was that she called to give me a warning.

"John was disappointed in you," she said. "He was disappointed you couldn't get him those pills."

"Yoko," I replied, "I never said they were pills. I told you they were injections."

"You told me you went to a doctor, and he gave you pills, and you lost weight," she insisted.

"With all due respect, that's not what I said . . ."

"It's very important that whenever you make a promise to John, you must keep it," she continued, ignoring my correction and giving me a piece of advice that would later turn out to be invaluable. "Don't promise John anything you can't fulfill. Never disappoint him. Because he has an issue with trust, with people being truthful."

As it turned out, I must not have disappointed him too much, because from that point on John started phoning me almost every day. And not just to discuss diet pills. Over those early weeks, our calls quickly branched off into gab sessions about politics, history, theology, and scores of other subjects. There were many conversations about books: John was always suggesting things for me to read and soon even started sending me literary care packages. I'd open my mailbox to find it filled with tomes he'd sent—not merely inscribed but frequently annotated in the margins with his hand-scribbled doodles—only to have him call the next day to ask if I'd finished reading them yet.

Of course, Yoko was also calling me every day, which meant that I was suddenly ears-deep in a three-way telephonic extravaganza. It was head spinning and exhilarating but also, frankly, enormously time-consuming. There were days when Yoko would wrap up a two-hour conversation by saying that John wanted to talk to me. Then she'd pass the phone along and I'd spend the next couple of hours on the line with him.

I still had something resembling a personal life: a radio show that required my attention, a dog that needed walking, neighbors who occasionally invited me to hang out. But more and more I could feel myself being split in two, like a reluctant superhero with a double identity. One Elliot Mintz was a mild-mannered radio talk show host; the other led a clandestine existence—John and Yoko's secret friend—that not even my closest pals knew about.

I remember, about six weeks after the radio interview with John, I attended one of Micky and Samantha Dolenz's epic holiday parties. Dolenz had used some of his Monkee money to purchase that sprawling house on Horse Shoe Canyon Road, a four-story Swiss chalet–like edifice that had been built in the 1930s by a Disney designer. Every November he and his wife would host a Thanksgiving dinner for what Samantha referred to as the Laurel Canyon orphans: folks who didn't have family in California or for whatever reason had no other place to go. They were lavish affairs, at least by the counterculture standards of the neighborhood. The tables were set with crystal glassware, not the usual jelly jars or paper cups, and there were cloth settings and silver flatware and bone china platters upon which were served a feast for the ages—not merely one turkey but four or five giant birds roasted to perfection in the ovens of their state-of-the-art 1970s kitchen.

Micky and I were becoming good buddies and he greeted me at his front door with a bear hug. "Everybody's still talking about your John Lennon interview," he said with a grin as he led me into his home. And he was right. As I chatted with other party guests—Donovan, Brian Wilson, Danny Hutton, Beau and Jeff Bridges—I was frequently grilled about those forty minutes on the radio. At one point Alice Cooper, another of the Laurel Canyon orphans, pulled me aside, wrapped an arm around my shoulders, and asked with almost childlike awe, "What was it like, Elliot? What was it like talking to John Lennon?"

"Like talking to an old friend" is all I could think to say.

I obviously didn't tell Cooper how earlier that very day I had spent a few hours engaged in an animated discussion with both John and Yoko, just as I had the day before, and the day before that. None of the people at that party—or anywhere else on earth, for that matter—had the slightest clue that my life was being increasingly consumed by two famous strangers who at this point I still hadn't even met in person.

But that last part was soon to change.

FOUR

Ojai, 1972

They were the sort of directions one might receive from a kidnapper.

"Drive three and a half miles until you see a large oak tree. Behind the tree, there's a field. Across the field, you'll see a pay phone. Drive around the field till you get to the phone. You'll see a green station wagon parked nearby . . ."

The voice on the other end of the phone dispensing these instructions was Peter Bendrey, aka "Peter the Dealer." A longtime member of John and Yoko's entourage, Peter performed several functions for the couple above and beyond the one hinted at by his nickname. For John, he was an all-around troubleshooter. For Yoko, he sometimes designed art catalogues for her gallery showings. At other times, though, he was also a chauffeur, which was the service he was engaged in when he gave me the directions to the phone booth across the hill behind the large oak tree.

But I'm getting ahead of myself. Let's back up a few weeks . . .

In late May of 1972, John and Yoko decided to take a cross-country road trip. Although they were both obviously familiar with New York and, to some degree, Los Angeles, most of what they had observed of what lay between the coasts had been from an altitude of 30,000 feet. So, to explore the fruited plain and mountain majesties from ground level, they piled into their enormous green Chrysler Town & Country station wagon—the "Dragon Wagon," it was called—and, with Peter the Dealer at the wheel, set out to look at America.

Truth be told, there was another, more pressing reason for the road trip. As John would tell me soon after we met, both John and Yoko were withdrawing from methadone, a drug they had fallen into after recent addictions to heroin. Kicking methadone was no walk in the park—some say it's even worse than heroin withdrawal. Throughout the trip, John and Yoko must have suffered a slew of symptoms—chills, fever, muscle aches, nausea, sweating, rapid heartbeat, irritability—but traveling with Peter no doubt provided some relief. Marijuana, it turned out, did wonders to alleviate the discomfort, and if there was one thing their driver knew how to procure, it was pot.

John had hinted vaguely that a trip out west might be in his and Yoko's future; he had mentioned it in passing in one of the notes he'd started mailing me around this time. But he hadn't kept me apprised of any details, and I wasn't aware they were already crossing the country. Their daily phone calls continued as usual, but they must have been placed from roadside motels or wherever else they spent their nights during their journey. It never occurred to me that they might be in California so soon, summoning me for our first in-person encounter.

So, when I picked up the phone at around noon on a Friday in June, just as I was stretching awake in bed, I was more than a little surprised to hear Peter on the other end of the line.

"John and Yoko want to see you," he said. "They're here. We just drove across country."

"Really?" I replied. "Um, that's great. When do they want to see me?"

"This afternoon."

"Of course. I'd be delighted!" I assumed the meeting would take place at a hotel in Los Angeles—the Beverly Wilshire, perhaps, or maybe the Beverly Hills Hotel—about fifteen minutes from Laurel Canyon. But then Peter started giving me directions to Ojai, a picturesque mountain town about eighty miles north of L.A.

I had no idea how or why John and Yoko had ended up in Ojai. I wondered if maybe Peter had taken a wrong turn off the Pomona Freeway. Or if the Lennons had decided to embark on a spiritual detour. In those days, before it became famous for its hot stone massages and other spa specialties, Ojai was a metaphysical retreat, a center for philosophical and transcendental contemplation. Indeed, J. Krishnamurti himself owned a home there.

In any case, I knew the area a little, having visited it on several occasions, which is why I was a bit alarmed by John and Yoko's choice of it as a meeting place: even with light traffic, it would take me at least ninety minutes to get there from Laurel Canyon, and even in the early 1970s, traffic was seldom light on a Friday afternoon in L.A. Also, being a Friday, I had a radio show to broadcast that night, which meant I had to be back in town by 9:00 p.m.

There was little time to waste.

I quickly threw on a pair of jeans and a Hawaiian shirt, descended to street level via the hillevator, climbed into my car— I'd recently jettisoned the Morris Minor and upgraded to an old white Jaguar sedan with a red interior and what would turn out to be an endless series of mechanical problems—and pointed it west towards the Pacific Coast Highway. This part of the trip didn't require Peter's elaborate kidnapper-style instructions: Just follow the PCH north and it's a straight shot to Ventura, then a right turn to Ojai. In fact, I knew the route well enough that I put myself on semi-autopilot, rolling down the window to enjoy the sea breeze as I glided up the coast.

I was, I must admit, a little nervous: partly because I was worried I wouldn't be able to follow Peter's convoluted directions once I arrived at Ojai's town limits, but also because I wasn't sure how the first physical exchange with John and Yoko would go. As close as the three of us had grown over the past eight months, it had been a relationship conducted entirely through copper telephone wires. Once I ceased to be merely a disembodied voice on the phone and became a real live corporeal entity, would the spell of our friendship grow less enchanting? Would the flesh-and-bone Elliot live up to their expectations?

After about an hour and forty-five minutes, I finally found my way to the oak tree. It was right where Peter had said it would be. I could see the phone booth across the field just as he said I would. I steered along the road that wrapped around the scruffy pasture till I came to the designated spot and—sure enough—parked nearby was their green station wagon.

Our moment had arrived.

I took a deep breath, stepped out of my car, and tentatively walked towards their vehicle. I noticed one of its rear doors opening and caught a glimpse of a slight female figure dressed from head to toe in black. Behind her, lounging in the back seat, was a taller, lankier-looking male with a long beard and tinted wire-framed glasses.

Yoko climbed out of the car, stood by its door, and, for the very first time, looked me up and down. I did the same to her. She was even shorter and thinner than I expected from her photographs, with her long black hair grazing the base of her spine.

"Go on, then," I heard John say from the back of the station wagon, "give 'im a hug."

Yoko, as I've mentioned before, was not a physically demonstrative person. But she stepped forward to engage in something sort of like a hug—let's call it a light tapping on my back. Then John jumped out of the car. He, it turned out, *was* a hugger. He wrapped his arms around me so tightly, I was a little startled.

John was no giant—he was about five feet ten inches—but I was considerably shorter and he towered over me as he tugged me into his chest.

"It's good to meet you."

After a few more perfunctory pleasantries, John instructed me to follow them to the house where they were staying. For reasons I didn't quite understand at the time, they seemed in a hurry to get back. So I slipped into my car and trailed the Dragon Wagon down some dusty, bumpy roads for about ten minutes till we pulled up to a remote house in the middle of nowhere.

It was a suburban-looking one-story affair with no landscaping, a couple of small bedrooms, a tiny kitchen, and, around back, a pint-sized pool with a diving board. I later learned that this otherwise nondescript home had a long, storied history: it had been built in 1905 by a Civil War veteran and had once been owned by a retired Vassar philosophy professor, but by the 1960s had been acquired by a leftist-leaning lawyer and his wife, who turned it into something of a "safe house" for anti-war radicals looking to lie low from the authorities.

"Are ya hungry?" John asked after we entered the house, the creaky screen door banging behind us.

"I could eat something," I replied. Aside from a banana on the way down the hillevator in Laurel Canyon, I hadn't had time for a bite all day.

"Help yourself," he said, pointing to the tiny kitchen before he followed Yoko out the back door to the pool.

There was nothing in the fridge. At least, nothing discernibly edible—just a few bottles of water and some containers filled with unidentifiable and unappetizing-looking substances that I presumed to be health food of some sort. One of the side effects of methadone withdrawal is loss of appetite, which might have explained why their kitchen was so poorly stocked. But as I got to know John and Yoko better over the years, I learned this was a perennial issue. They had unconventional tastes and seldom kept anything that appeared appetizing in their refrigerators.

After poking around for a bit, I grabbed a bottle of water and headed outside to the pool, where I found myself standing in something like a still from a Fellini movie. Yoko, in a black one-piece swimsuit and wraparound sunglasses, was lying on her back on the diving board, looking straight up into the sky. Her hair was dangling down from the board, hovering an inch or so above the waterline. She seemed so motionless, it was almost surreal, as if time itself had frozen, but also somehow heart-achingly beautiful. I couldn't take my eyes off her.

Then I heard some fidgeting behind me.

"Just changing into me swimming costume," John shouted from behind a folding bamboo screen. "A little shy, ya know."

What emerged a moment later was one of the palest human beings I had ever seen. Honestly, John's skin was almost as white as Xerox paper.

The three of us (I had no idea where Peter had gone off to) sat by the pool for a few minutes, basking silently in the sunlight. I kept waiting for a conversation to start, but for some reason

John and Yoko seemed intent on remaining quiet. It was getting awkward—weird, even—so I decided to say something, but before I could think of what that something might be, Yoko abruptly got up from the diving board and walked over to where John and I were sitting in vinyl chairs. She bent down to my ear.

"Follow me," she whispered, then turned and headed inside.

I looked at John, puzzled. He just nodded, so I got up and did as I was asked.

Yoko led me down a narrow hallway into a bathroom and turned the faucet on in the tub—not to fill it up, just to make some noise. Then she sat on the edge and motioned for me to join her.

"This house is bugged," she said so softly I had to strain to hear her. "Everything we say is being recorded. They're listening to everything." She leaned in closer. "You must not repeat anything we say to you. It's very dangerous. Don't even tell people you know us, or they could start listening or following you."

"But, Yoko," I whispered back, "why would 'they' pay attention to me? I pose no threat . . ."

"All kinds of people want to know what we do and where we go," she said impatiently. "We are very careful of who we trust. Everyone betrays us. Just keep us your secret."

It was the first time either of them had made the clandestine nature of our friendship explicit, although it was hardly the first time I'd heard them fret about being surveilled. John had mentioned it on numerous occasions, interrupting our phone conversations to point out a clicking sound on the line—proof, in his mind, that J. Edgar Hoover's agents were listening in. I once made the mistake of pointing out that if the government wanted to bug their phones, the technology must have existed to do so without making telltale clicking noises. My skepticism enraged John so much, he fumed about it for days. I quickly learned never to do that again.

But sitting on the edge of the tub with Yoko, trying to decipher her whispers through the din of the running water, I had to wonder if perhaps their otherwise understandable suspicions might be verging on paranoia. It was difficult for me to imagine an advance team of dark-suited FBI agents sneaking into this house in Ojai and planting listening devices around its swimming pool. It was even harder for me to conceive of them bugging the likes of me, a harmless radio talk show host in L.A. Surely, the U.S. government had better things to do with its time.

Of course, as I would later learn, it wasn't paranoia at all. John and Yoko were indeed being surveilled, although maybe not at this time and place in Ojai. A Freedom of Information Act lawsuit filed in the mid-1980s would turn up hundreds of pages of secret files on John and Yoko, most of them compiled during the late 1960s and early 1970s, when President Nixon got it into his head that the Lennons were a threat to national security—or at least to his reelection plans for 1972.

John and Yoko's anti–Vietnam War activism—particularly their headline-grabbing bed-ins—were no doubt a thorn in Nixon's side. After all, the battle here at home was to win the hearts and minds (and votes) of the American people, and John and

Yoko's public demonstrations were proving to be powerful artillery in the fight for peace. But that's not all that got Nixon worked up. There had been intel that John and Yoko were planning on crashing and disrupting the 1972 Republican convention in Florida, potentially creating an embarrassing spectacle rivaling the Democrats' disastrous convention four years earlier in Chicago. That, Nixon couldn't allow; he instructed the FBI to dig up something incriminating on John, some dirt that could be used as a pretext for having him deported back to the UK.

In truth, John had no plans to disrupt Nixon's renomination. Yes, he and Yoko had been spending time with anti-war activists like Jerry Rubin and Abbie Hoffman, who had glommed on to the couple the moment they moved to New York. And, yes, Rubin and Hoffman did indeed concoct a plan to send John and Yoko to the Florida convention. But that was never going to happen. John was no partisan; he distrusted politicians of every persuasion and hardly ever got involved in campaigns. "I've never voted in me life," he once admitted to me, "and I've never told anyone how to vote."

John's ideology, from what I could tell from our months of telephone conversations, was more of a loose consortium of ideas and concepts—some of which, at the time, might have seemed radical to the Nixon crowd—than any sort of organized creed. He was pro free love and was a supporter of feminism and abortion rights. He fervently felt that marijuana should be legalized. But above all else, he believed that the world should "give peace a chance," as he so eloquently put it in the chant that would become the anthem for the anti-war movement.

Beyond that, it was hard to pin him down to any specific political agenda.

He was John Lennon, the guy who imagined a world of peace and love; *those* were his politics.

IF that afternoon in Ojai *had* been recorded by the FBI—and there was no evidence in any of the files retrieved by that Freedom of Information Act lawsuit that it was—all the government would have heard was a very pleasant conversation among three close friends meeting each other for the first time. Whatever apprehensions I had leading up to the encounter quickly melted as we chatted by the pool, every bit as comfortable with one another as we had been on the phone. Indeed, despite John and Yoko's certainty that we were being recorded by the FBI, they eventually ended up being quite gabby.

At one point, after Yoko slipped into the house for a moment, John leaned forward to offer me a word of wisdom about his spouse.

"Listen, mate," he said in hushed tones, "here's the thing you need to know about Mother. She's going to tell you things that make no sense. She's going to ask you to do things that sound fuckin' crazy. There will be times when you'll think she's bloody mad. Just do what she tells you to do. She's almost always right. She sees things other people can't see."

I nodded, even though I didn't appreciate at the time what golden advice he was giving me. Then I changed the subject.

"Do you think you could ever live in Ojai full-time? Or some other rural place? Could you live outside of a big city?" I inquired.

"Never," he quickly replied. "Mother is an ocean child; that's literally what her name translates to in English. And I came from a city on the water. Liverpool flows through me blood. And New York stimulates me creatively, although it sometimes makes me crazy. We're here to get away and get clean but I can't wait to get the fuck out."

As with all my conversations with John and Yoko, time seemed to fold in on itself, and before I knew it, the sky had taken on an amaranthine glow as the sun began its slow slide to the horizon. It was nearing 7:00 p.m., and I needed to head back to L.A. for my radio show. I quickly said my goodbyes and started to gather myself for the drive back down the PCH, but just as I was about to get into my car, John stopped me in the driveway.

"We've got a little present for you," he said with a huge grin, motioning Yoko to me. She pressed an acetate record into my hands. There were no markings on its cardboard sleeve. The recording was so fresh, its artwork and liner notes hadn't yet been printed. There was simply a hand-scribbled inscription on the label: "To Elliot. Much love from John Lennon and Yoko Ono." It was dated June 9 but John had somehow gotten the year wrong, writing 1971.

"It's our new album," he continued. "It's called *Some Time in New York City*. Nobody's heard it yet. We haven't given it to anyone. We wanted you to have it. Maybe you can play it on the radio tonight?"

This was no "little present"—this was an incredible honor. John and Yoko were handing me a first pressing of the album they'd been collaborating on together for the better half of a year and allowing me the privilege of dropping it on my show. I was speechless.

I had no idea what was on the album and no way to listen to it while racing back to L.A. Nevertheless, by the time I burst into my studio booth at the radio station with just minutes to spare before going on the air, I had made the decision to play the entire thing live and uninterrupted. It seemed like a no-brainer. After all, I had the jump on the whole broadcast world: the first crack at John and Yoko's latest album.

"Ladies and gentlemen, I'm going to get some advertisements out of the way and then for the next hour you're in for a treat," I announced over the airwaves. "We're going to play a brand-new album by John Lennon and Yoko Ono and we're all going to experience it for the first time together."

A few minutes later, when we came out of commercial breaks, I cued my engineer behind the glass wall to drop the tone arm onto the acetate.

It took me all of fifteen seconds to realize I was in big trouble. When John started crooning the n-word on the record's first track—a proto-feminist screed titled "Woman Is the N—— of the World"—I saw my engineer's jaw drop. We stared at each other in shocked panic. But there was no way to stop now. After promising listeners the full album, uninterrupted by commercials, we just had to play the rest of the record, wincing through songs about the Attica State Prison riot ("Free the prisoners, jail the judges"), the jailing of Marxist college professor Angela Davis ("Angela, you're one of the millions / Of political prisoners in the world"), and the British colonial rule of Ireland ("land full of beauty and wonder / . . . raped by the British brigands").

John and Yoko weren't actual bomb-throwing radicals, but they certainly knew how to toss a musical Molotov cocktail into the cultural zeitgeist. *Some Time in New York City* was one of the most politically incendiary albums I'd ever heard.

In general, when it came to politics, John was less interested in promoting specific issues than in the broader picture— promoting peace and love. So, this was a huge change, and a total surprise to me, especially coming from two people I thought I knew so well. To my knowledge, not only had John and Yoko never recorded songs like this, but no one else had, either. Not that I thought it was a mistake for them to record it; I understood where they were coming from—they wanted people to know about Attica, about Davis and Ireland. When they had feelings, they expressed them. And they certainly expressed them here.

But that didn't make that particular day any easier. When the record was finally over, I suspected my career was, too. It was a long drive home at two in the morning.

Sure enough, the next day I was called into the station manager's office.

"We're going in a different direction with your time slot," he told me. He didn't need to explain further; I knew that direction didn't include me behind a mic. When I returned home, freshly unemployed, the first thing I did was pick up the phone and call John.

"Well," I said, "I've got some good news and some bad news."

"What's the good?" he asked.

"I played your entire album without any commercial breaks last night."

"Fuckin' great!" he shouted. I heard him repeat the news to Yoko, who must have been nearby. "Mother, he played the whole record last night—the whole record!"

"The bad news," I went on, "is that I'm out of a job."

There was a beat as John processed this information. Then he burst out laughing. "And, Mother—they fired him!" I heard him yell to Yoko. I could hear her laughing, too.

Naturally, I was less amused. I liked my job. I liked radio. I liked getting a paycheck. But suddenly I was on the skids. I had no idea if I'd ever work in broadcasting again.

After he finally stopped laughing, John asked, "So, what are you going to do now?"

"I don't have any immediate plans," I answered icily.

"Well then," he said, "why don't you come back up to Ojai. We're going to drive on to San Francisco. Come with us, Ellie. Join the circus!"

What else could I do?

I said yes.

PART TWO

MAGICAL MYSTERY TOUR

FIVE

San Francisco, 1972

M emory is a curious thing.

Even today, all these years later, I can vividly recall John's voice on the phone—his lilting Liverpool accent, the silly dialects he would sometimes put on when he was feeling happy, his clenched tone when he was not—as if I'd hung up with him only minutes ago. If I close my eyes, pinch the bridge of my nose, and concentrate a bit harder, I can reconstruct complete conversations we had decades in the past, the memories rushing over me as if I'd just bitten into a Proustian pot brownie.

And yet, for some reason, try as I might, I cannot recall exactly how I got from Laurel Canyon to Ojai to join John and Yoko on their road trip to San Francisco. I didn't drive my newly purchased, mechanically impaired Jaguar: I wouldn't have parked and left it unattended while we all piled into the Dragon Wagon for what would turn out to be a weeks-long trip. I don't recall if

I took a train or bus to Ojai. Did I rent a car? My memory of that moment is about as precise as a pocket watch drooping over a tree branch.

No matter. What I *do* distinctly remember, with crystal clarity, is sitting up front in the station wagon next to Peter, with John and Yoko sprawled in the back, barreling up the PCH towards the Golden City as "The Loco-Motion" blared at top volume from John's eccentric mobile stereo system.

"*I know you're gonna like it if you give it a chance now . . .* ," Little Eva crooned through the car's speaker system. "*My little baby sister can do it with ease.*"

Remember, this was 1972. The cassette deck had been introduced as an automobile accessory three years earlier. The 8-track had been available in cars since 1965. But for some reason, the Dragon Wagon had been tricked out with a turntable that played only 45s. It was mounted under the dash, to the right of the driver's seat, and it was a less-than-dependable piece of machinery. If the Dragon Wagon hit even a small road bump, the needle on the weighted arm would skip on the vinyl.

Still, John loved the thing. He'd sit in the back with a stack of singles—"Long Tall Sally" ("*She's built for speed, she got / Everything that Uncle John need*"); "Whole Lotta Shakin' Going On" ("*We ain't fakin' / Whole lot of shakin' goin' on*"); "Don't Be Cruel" ("*If you can't come around / At least please telephone*")—and pass them up to Peter, who'd slip them on the turntable like a human jukebox.

The loud music made conversation during the car ride challenging. I'd have to twist around to face John in the back seat and holler my questions or comments over whatever tune was playing. Incredibly, Yoko seemed to sleep through most of it, her head resting against the window.

"Always loved this one!" I yelled when Rosie and the Originals started singing their 1960 hit "Angel Baby."

John nodded in agreement.

Rosie chimed in on the speakers: *"It's just like heaven being here with you."*

"I think Rosie Hamlin wrote and recorded it when she was just fourteen," I went on.

"Yeah, she made it in a garage somewhere near L.A. on a two-track and couldn't get anyone to listen to it," he shouted back. "And some fuckin' hustlers stole it from her and kept the cash."

"It happened a lot in those days," I said.

John looked me straight in the eyes. "You don't have to tell me, Angel Baby," he said. "It happened to us." He was referring, I realized, to the Beatles' fraught publishing arrangement with Northern Songs, the music publishing company that for a time lorded over the Beatles catalogue.

"You're like an angel, too good to be true," Rosie sang on.

Later, while Steppenwolf boomed "Born to Be Wild" on the turntable, I tried my luck talking with Peter. He wasn't exactly the chatty type—interpersonal skills were not his strong suit— but at least I didn't have to shout as loudly since he was sitting at the wheel right next to me.

"Did they play music most of the time while you were driving across the country?" I asked.

"Sometimes," he replied, munching on some trail mix he kept in a baggie next to him. "Sometimes they spoke with each other or just slept."

"It's amazing Yoko is able to sleep now," I said as Goldy McJohn's soaring keyboard riffs filled the station wagon.

"Oh, she's not sleeping," he said with a smile. "She's just got her eyes closed."

About three hours into the drive, as we approached Big Sur, John told Peter to look for a spot near the beach where we could stop.

"I need to stretch me legs," he pronounced.

A few minutes later, we pulled into a nearly vacant lot overlooking some dunes. Except for a few surfers bobbing in the waves, the strand was completely empty. So the four of us climbed out of the car and walked across the sand to the shoreline. Yoko was wrapped in a black silk shawl with scarves fluttering behind her in the breeze; she looked like a Bedouin in the Sahara. John wasn't merely stretching his legs; he was twirling and pirouetting in the sand, performing a barefoot modern dance number to a tune he alone could hear. Peter, meanwhile, was standing with his back to the wind, his fingers fiddling with something that turned out to be an enormous joint.

Yoko never smoked pot—she hated the smell. The drugs she preferred, when she was doing drugs, were usually of the odorless variety, like cocaine, pills, or heroin. John, on the other hand, enjoyed pot very much, often multiple times a day. After Peter lit the doobie—not an easy task on a windy beach—he passed it to John, who took a long, impressive drag, then handed it to me. I examined Peter's handiwork, a little jealous of his prodigious joint-rolling abilities, took a tentative toke, and nearly coughed my lungs out. Peter's weed was a much more potent strain of cannabis than the borderline oregano I smoked back home in Laurel Canyon. Also, I hadn't eaten in what felt like days—John and Yoko, still withdrawing from methadone, showed no interest in stopping at any of the restaurants or diners we had passed along the way—and the smoke went straight to my head.

So, yes, you could say I got high with a little help from my friends.

I didn't suddenly hear imaginary sitar music or hallucinate dragons in the sky; as powerful as it was, it was pot, not acid. But it did instill in me a heightened awareness of my surroundings— the briny taste of the sea air, the rhythmic beat of the ceaseless waves—and reframed my consciousness about the universe and my infinitesimally tiny place in it. That helped put things in perspective.

I was out of a job. I had no idea when or where my next one would come from. My bank account would soon be depleted. And yet, twirling and laughing with John on this empty beach in Big Sur as Yoko stood by smiling, I felt an overwhelming sense of contentment and belonging. Although I wasn't fully aware of it at the time, looking back now, fifty years later, it may well have been one of the happiest moments of my life.

After thirty or forty minutes of frolicking, John signaled that it was time to resume our journey, so we all filed across the beach and piled back into the car. John kissed Yoko on the forehead and wrapped a light blanket around her as she leaned against him in the back seat. After Peter swung the Dragon back onto PCH, John handed him another 45, and we all listened in stoned silence to Procol Harum's "A Whiter Shade of Pale."

"*We skipped the light fandango*," Gary Brooker droned soulfully from the speakers, singing words that have confounded generations of rock 'n' roll fans. "*Turned cartwheels 'cross the floor.*"

When it was over, I turned towards the back and asked John if he knew what the song meant.

"What do you mean, what the song meant?" he replied.

"I mean what the lyrics are about."

"No," he said. "That's not the way I listen to music. It's like 'Tutti Frutti': What do those lyrics mean? It's about the rhythm, the chord changes, and the backbeat. That's what makes me feel a song."

"I get that," I said. "But *Some Time in New York City* is certainly about more than just the backbeat. It's also about what you are thinking and feeling."

John seemed a little annoyed at this line of questioning. He was not a fan of dissecting his own work.

"That's because of Yoko," he said. "She's the one who's always encouraging me to shout about me fuckin' feelings."

Yoko chimed in: "Elliot, can't you see that John has never had the opportunity to speak what he was feeling? His teachers didn't understand him. His auntie burnt his poetry. Other people manipulated his life. So now, for the first time, he's free to express himself and his true feelings."

That's when John expressed a true feeling that I myself had been struggling with for the whole ride. "I could do with a spot to eat," he said.

I silently thanked the heavens—I was starving—and mentioned that we were only about thirty minutes from Monterey's Fisherman's Wharf, where I knew there were a slew of restaurants. The second I suggested it, though, I realized it was a terrible idea: they were John Lennon and Yoko Ono. They couldn't pop up on a crowded pier without any security. Things could quickly get dangerous. But John waved away my concerns.

"Don't you worry, Ellie," he said with a grin. "Let's get to this pier."

"Ellie" was the first nickname John gave me, but it was far from the last. As I was about to learn, he was always creating different characters, both for me and for himself. And they could come from anywhere. Several years later, John was preparing some food and he brought out this beautiful, large wok and started to cook vegetables. And I just matter-of-factly said, "That's a great wok." And that became a nickname and another character for him: "The Great Wok."

As Peter headed north towards Monterey, John and Yoko started behaving strangely. They began whispering to each other in the back seat. After a while their whispering grew more intense, then turned into a mantra or something like a Hare

Krishna chant. I couldn't quite make out the words they were intoning—it sounded a little like "Free to workin'," maybe, or "Friday lurkin'." I glanced over to Peter. He seemed unfazed, so I had to assume this was not unusual John and Yoko behavior. I shrugged and decided to let it go.

When we got to the wharf, my heart sank: there must have been five hundred tourists packed onto the pier. There was no way John and Yoko could navigate such a huge throng without getting mobbed. Before I could raise any objections, though, the two of them were already out the doors and heading from the parking lot straight into the crowd. I dashed after them while Peter, who remained weirdly unconcerned, stayed behind in the Wagon, nibbling on his trail mix while keeping an eye on our belongings.

I was close to panicking as I elbowed through the tourists and tried to catch up to John and Yoko. I could see them just ahead, casually weaving through the crowd as they strolled past the scores of busy gift shops and ice-cream parlors and whale-watching businesses that filled the wharf's promenade. I kept expecting the worst: a crushing upheaval once people recognized who was among them. But remarkably, miraculously, that didn't happen.

The most recognizable couple on the planet had ambled smack into the middle of a horde of hundreds, and not a single soul seemed to know who they were. I couldn't understand it. How was this possible?

When I caught up with them, I quickly steered us towards a

lobster restaurant at the end of the wharf. I'd eaten there before on a previous trip to Monterey and recalled it being dimly lit. We were lucky and found a relatively secluded table towards the back of the dining room. Once we settled into our seats, I shot them both an inquisitive stare.

"How?" was all I said.

John smiled, then explained what I had just witnessed.

It seemed that John and Yoko had developed a bizarre but apparently remarkably effective method of crowd control. It involved some sort of esoteric mind game in which they each mentally disguised themselves with alternative identities: John became the Reverend Fred Gherkin and Yoko became his wife, Ada. That's what they'd been chanting in the back of the Wagon a few moments earlier: "Fred and Ada Gherkin." Somehow, as improbable as it sounds, John and Yoko took on these imaginary roles so completely and authentically that they were able to project them to the outside world. Like a sort of mass-hypnosis invisibility cloak, it rendered them all but undetectable.

"Works every time!" John said as he unfurled a napkin on his lap. Yoko nodded in agreement.

Indeed, it did work. Or at least it did until it didn't.

When the waiter came over to take our orders, he, too, seemed bewitched by the Fred and Ada Gherkin enchantment. Then John ordered a piece of fish. You could see the veils fall from our server's eyes the moment he heard John's voice.

"This is such an honor, Mr. Lennon," he gushed nervously. "I've loved you since I saw the Beatles on *The Ed Sullivan Show.*"

He fumbled with his pen and asked John to sign a napkin. As John jotted down his autograph, you could sense a shift in the air. Suddenly, with the Gherkin magic collapsing, all eyes were on our table. We could hear murmurs of John's and Yoko's names filling the room and the scraping of chairs as people got up from their tables to approach ours.

More napkins and pens were thrust in front of John, who did his best to accommodate his intrusive fans. But I could tell both he and Yoko were growing deeply uncomfortable. I was feeling nervous, too. I told the waiter to cancel our order and nodded to John and Yoko that we should make a hasty retreat before things got even more out of control.

Outside the restaurant, it was just as bad: suddenly everyone on the wharf seemed acutely aware of John and Yoko's presence. Most people were polite; they simply wanted to express their gratitude for John's music, to reach out and touch their idol's arm. Still, it was suffocating, and I did my best to gently push John and Yoko through the crowd, desperate to reach the safety of the station wagon waiting for us in the parking lot.

A few minutes later, after we had made our escape and Peter was once again steering us towards San Francisco, I turned to John and Yoko and asked him what went wrong. Why had the Gherkin disguise failed them?

"It's me voice," he said, sounding dejected. "That's what broke the spell. People always knew me voice before they knew what I looked like."

For the next couple of hours, we drove in silence. Yoko napped—or seemed to—with her head resting on John's shoulder. John stared out the window, mesmerized by the sun setting on the ocean's horizon. I listened to my stomach growl. By the time we arrived at the Miyako, a Japanese-themed hotel where John and Yoko sometimes stayed when visiting San Francisco, it was around nine in the evening. We were all hungry, tired, and ready to call it a night.

But when we tried to check in, the hotel clerk couldn't find our reservations.

John and Yoko's accommodations were arranged by a travel agent in New York, who always used pseudonyms for their bookings. It was a standard arrangement for celebrities, a precaution to protect their privacy. Except this time John and Yoko couldn't remember what pseudonym they had picked.

Normally, Peter would check them in, but he was outside in the car, keeping an eye on all our luggage. John and Yoko were standing quietly in a corner of the hotel lobby, staring very closely at a painting on the wall. This was another of their crowd control mind games: they believed they could avoid attention if they simply turned their backs and pretended to study an object in the room. It kind of worked, but it left me to sort out matters with the keeper of the keys, acting as John and Yoko's unofficial assistant, the first but hardly last time I'd assume that role.

"Perhaps it's under our driver's name?" I suggested to the man behind the desk. "Do you have anything under 'Bendrey, Peter'?"

"No, I'm afraid not," the clerk said after flipping through a stack of reservation cards.

"What about 'Mintz, Elliot'?"

"No, sir, not under that name, either."

I thought for a moment.

"How about the 'Reverend Fred Gherkin'?"

He shuffled through the cards and yanked one out with a flourish.

"Yes! I've got four rooms reserved for the Reverend," he said, pulling some paperwork for me to sign. "Why didn't you ask for that name in the first place?"

THE Miyako was an unusual little hotel located at the base of Pacific Heights, in San Francisco's Japantown. The main appeal to John and Yoko was that it was a low-key, out-of-the-way destination that nobody paid much attention to. They could cross its lobby with much less of a chance of being recognized than if they stayed at, say, the Fairmont, where the press would catch on to their presence before their luggage had even made it up the elevator.

But the Miyako was also a hotel that complemented John and Yoko's lifestyle in other ways. Half the rooms were decorated in traditional Japanese style, with tatami mats and futon mattresses and shoji screens. The rooms in the other half were adorned with a more Western touch—box spring beds and overstuffed sofas—although even in these there were still plenty of Asian influences, including a room service menu that featured authentic Japanese cuisine. Best of all, at least from my hungry point of view, the Miyako's kitchen stayed open late. First thing I did after escorting "Fred and Ada" to their rooms was order up a sushi feast, which the three of us shared in their suite. Peter, as usual, had disappeared to wherever he disappeared to.

"Listen, Ellie," John said as he and Yoko picked at their food, "there's something we need to tell ya. There's a reason Mother and me came to San Francisco. We've got something to do here. You probably won't be seeing us all that much."

I nodded as I shoveled sashimi into my mouth. "Okay," I mumbled between bites. "Is it something I can help you with?"

"No, Elliot," Yoko said. "This is not something you can help us with."

There was an awkward pause while John and Yoko exchanged glances. Then they proceeded to share with me their true motive for driving up to San Francisco: they wanted to have a baby.

John, of course, already had a child, Julian, with his ex-wife, Cynthia. Before his death, John would forge a closer relationship with his firstborn, but at this time, in 1972, he was still deeply estranged from his then nine-year-old son. John's divorce from Cynthia and his very public love affair with Yoko had all but shattered their father-son bond.

Yoko also had a child, Kyoko, with her ex-husband Anthony Cox. Since their divorce, Cox had become a devout born-again Christian who believed that Yoko and her new husband's "radical" lifestyle was a threat to Kyoko's well-being. So he abducted the child when she was just seven years old and spent the next several decades hiding out with her in "safe houses" run by fringe religious sects. Eventually, in 1998, when Yoko was sixty-five and Kyoko thirty-one, mother and daughter would finally be reunited. But before then Yoko and John spent many fruitless years and thousands of wasted dollars trying to track her down. Their current lack of relationships with both children were a source of great sadness for them and one I'd learn much more about over the years.

At the current moment, as they explained to me in their suite at the Miyako, John and Yoko desperately wanted a child together but had so far been unable to carry one to term. Indeed, Yoko had suffered multiple miscarriages since John and she had started trying. That was what had brought them to San Francisco: they had heard of a Chinese herbalist, Yuan Bain Hong, who supposedly performed fertility miracles with his patients. Yoko and John would be undergoing treatments with Hong for however long it took, and it would likely take some time.

When they finished unpacking all this, I put down my chopsticks and gave them a long, appreciative gaze. As close as we'd become over the last eight or nine months, this felt to me like a new level of friendship. I was touched that they had trusted me enough to share such an intimate and painful part of their lives.

"I completely understand," I said. "I hope this expert can help you."

As predicted, I didn't see a whole lot of John and Yoko during the following weeks in San Francisco. Or, for that matter, Peter, who was always driving the Lennons or off running some sort of errand for them. At one point John and Yoko moved into Hong's house in nearby San Mateo, spending several days under his care. Then they decamped for suburban Mill Valley, where they rented a strange circular house with no right angles that Peter had arranged through a friend.

"It's like living in a windmill," John said. "And I've always wanted to live in a windmill."

I stayed on at the Miyako, having grown fond of the place, particularly its spa, where I'd discovered the delights of Japanese massage. John and Yoko were generous, covering my hotel room, the massages, and all my expenses during the trip, all paid for with Yoko's credit card; John was terrible with money. And at the time, I was between jobs for reasons they knew very well, so I accepted gratefully and started to explore the city beyond Japantown. And there was so much to see: back in the early '70s, San Francisco was still the counterculture's unofficial capital. Strolling through Haight-Ashbury, I saw hippies playing lutes and tambourines as gaggles of colorfully adorned girls—literally wearing flowers in their hair, just like in the Scott McKenzie song—danced in the streets.

John and Yoko believed Hong helped them with their fertility issues—they told me as much. And over the next few weeks, whenever John and Yoko resurfaced from the doctor's treatments, they appeared in better health, stronger and more energetic—particularly John. Either Hong's potions were doing wonders, or else John and Yoko were finally putting the methadone withdrawal behind them. Whatever it was, it was great to see.

One afternoon at the Miyako, John called while I was in my room.

"What are ya doing?" he asked.

"I'm reading *The Fountainhead* by Ayn Rand," I told him.

"Why would you do that? Bloody bourgeois garbage for people with big heads and small balls."

"I found a copy in the lobby last night. I couldn't sleep, so I just picked it up for some bedtime reading. No reason for concern."

"Mother has an appointment. Why don't we go out. There's that famous paperback writer's bookstore. Let's pay that a little visit."

John was referring to City Lights, the celebrated independent bookshop in San Francisco that was famous for being the literary mecca of the bohemian scene. It certainly lived up to its reputation. As we walked in the door, I noticed the scene was unquestionably beatnik, filled with goatees, black turtlenecks, and even a few berets. John was immediately recognized, but this particular crowd was far too cool to react, and I was grateful that most of the patrons were going to leave John alone.

Most but not all.

"Pardon me for intruding, but aren't you and your wife friends with Allen Ginsberg?" a tweedy fellow in his sixties asked John as they both poked around the same stack of anthologies by

Lawrence Ferlinghetti. Apparently, to this gentleman, the most notable thing about John Lennon was that he had once hung out with the poet who wrote "Howl" and who sometimes played the pump organ while reciting his work.

"Yeah, Yoko and Allen go back to the sixties," John politely responded.

"What's he like in person?" the man asked.

"Same guy as you read about in his books. Only without the harmonium."

We lingered at the store for about thirty minutes, John filling a small basket with his selections, until we found ourselves at the cash register.

"I don't have any money," he told me. "You'll have to pay. You'll get it back in good karma." John seldom carried cash and seemed almost oblivious to money, but after all of their generosity I could hardly complain about the cost of a few books.

During the cab ride to the hotel, John vented about the bookstore. He was clearly in one of his moods. "Did you hear that guy ask about Ginsberg?" he fumed. "Bloody hell. Me books are as good as anything in that store. You ever read any of me books?"

"Of course," I replied. We'd talked about both of them—*In His Own Write* and *A Spaniard in the Works*—during several of our phone calls.

"Did ya notice none of me books were on the bloody shelves?"

"It's possible they were sold out," I suggested.

"Don't jerk me around with your radio voice diplomacy. They

weren't there because all those old farts still see me as a fuckin' mop top. That's the reason I didn't get any attention as a poet— because I was a bloody Beatle. But an artist is an artist, no matter what the medium."

At a red light, the cabdriver turned around. "I thought that might have been you when I picked you up," he said to John. "My wife's a big fan. Do you think you could sign this"—he held out a small piece of paper—"to Sylvia?"

"Tell your wife you made a mistake," John said, ignoring the paper.

Luckily, we were only a block from the Miyako. I gave the taxi driver a tip that was bigger than the fare.

In the lobby, John handed me his bag of books. "These are for you," he said. "I thought you needed something to take your mind off Ayn Rand." Then he disappeared for another couple of days, resuming the therapies with Hong.

FOR sure, San Francisco was a delightful diversion after getting fired from my radio job; however, after two weeks at the Miyako, I started thinking about heading home to Laurel Canyon. I had to find a new gig in L.A., and I needed to retrieve Shane from a neighbor, who'd agreed to take care of him for what I originally thought would just be a five-day trip. But before I left town, there was one more thing I wanted to do.

Truth be told, I had an ulterior motive of my own for coming to San Francisco that had nothing to do with visiting bookstores or girl-watching in Haight-Ashbury or even sharing face time with John and Yoko. It was something that had been occupying my mind from the moment John invited me to join the circus and come with them on their road trip.

Her name was Louise.

We'd met years earlier, bumping into each other in line at Canter's Deli in West Hollywood, which may not sound like a terribly romantic spot for a "meet-cute" encounter, but it had a certain L.A. charm. I was maybe twenty-one, finishing up at City College and starting out in radio. She was seventeen or eighteen, with long blond hair, doe eyes, and a smile so captivating it almost made me forgot what sort of sandwich I wanted to order.

Our affair was intense, as first loves tend to be, but also not very stable, which is also typical of puppy love. I was too wrapped up in forging a career for myself and she was too young to have any patience for a neglectful boyfriend, so we went our separate ways, or at least tried to. Somehow, though, we couldn't make the breakup stick. We kept circling back to each other, then breaking up again, boomeranging back and forth in an on-again, off-again arrangement that drove us both a little crazy. Eventually, we settled into what would ultimately become a decades-long platonic friendship, but it would take years for the romantic embers to completely fizzle out, if they ever fully did.

As it happened, Louise now lived in Mill Valley. So, as I'd been planning the whole trip, I called and invited her out to dinner . . . with my friends.

It was, in my mind, a simple experiment. I wanted to see if I could somehow find an intersection in the Venn diagram that was becoming my life. In one circle, there was my secret friendship with John and Yoko. In the other, everything else: my job, my neighbors and friends, my romantic partners, my increasingly fleeting downtime. Louise, I decided, would test whether there was a space in which the two separate universes could ever overlap.

It was, obviously, a gross violation of the rules that Yoko had only weeks earlier laid down in that bathroom in Ojai: "Don't even tell people you know us. Just keep us your secret." But I'd dropped Louise's name to John and Yoko more than once during our phone calls. So, when I casually suggested to them that I bring her to dinner, they didn't immediately shut down the idea. As much as they were suspicious of outsiders, I suppose a small part of them may have been somewhat curious about the only girl in my life I had ever bothered to mention to them.

We met at Soupçon, a tiny storefront-style café on Caledonia Street in Sausalito that Louise recommended. It wasn't fancy; there were only about ten tables and I think the most expensive dish on the menu was a crab salad for $6. Louise lived humbly and frugally; she wasn't one for fancy restaurants. But she wasn't the slightest bit starstruck. She spoke to John and Yoko as if they were just regular folk from out of town. John and Yoko, for their part, were friendly and courteous, if not exactly warm, but also kind of peculiar.

"If you ever marry this fellow, make certain he cleans the

dishes and takes the trash to the bin" was the first thing John said to Louise. He was joking, of course, but it struck me as an inelegant way to say hello.

"What do you usually eat here?" Yoko asked Louise while perusing the menu.

"I usually have the lentil soup," she replied.

"I will have that," Yoko declared, slapping closed the menu.

"Same for me," John said.

I looked around the table, feeling a bit like the chaperone of a reluctant blind date. "That's it?" I asked. "That's all you're ordering?"

Nobody said anything, so I ordered the soup, too. And a glass of Chardonnay.

Over the next forty minutes, the conversation was pleasant and polite but not particularly memorable. Mostly we talked about the food. The liveliest moment was during dessert; John couldn't decide what he wanted, so he ended up ordering everything from the dessert tray. I could tell Louise was overwhelmed.

By the end of the evening, though, I knew my little experiment had failed. John and Yoko never said as much out loud, but I could feel from their body language and the uneasiness of the small talk—as well as the meaningfully cool glances Yoko threw at me towards the end of the dinner—that they weren't at all thrilled I had brought an interloper into our midst.

Whatever magic happened between me, Yoko, and John when we got together, it couldn't be re-created as a party of four.

SIX

Laurel Canyon, 1972

had two telephone lines at my house in Laurel Canyon: one for personal calls, the other for business. But when I returned from San Francisco, I realized I needed a third.

I needed a John and Yoko hotline.

In those days, having a phone installed was not all that easy. You'd have to get a Ma Bell technician to come to your home, drill holes in your walls, lay cables along the edges of your baseboards, and hook up a landline handset. At the time, a chunky rotary-dial phone weighed about two and a half pounds and could travel only as far as its cord permitted. In my case, the installation was even more involved, because in addition to a third phone number I also wanted a red light fixed onto my bedroom ceiling that would flash whenever my new hotline rang.

"You're expecting calls from the White House?" the phone

installer cracked when I explained the unusual request. I resisted the temptation to tell him the truth, which would have sounded every bit as unlikely: "No, I need the red light so I don't miss any middle-of-the-night calls from John Lennon and Yoko Ono."

After I left San Francisco, hopping a quick flight back to L.A., John and Yoko lingered there a while longer, returning to New York in August—by commercial jet, not the Dragon Wagon, which Peter presumably drove back east himself—to headline at the One to One benefit concert at Madison Square Garden. That concert—organized by Geraldo Rivera to help the developmentally disabled child victims of the then infamous Willowbrook State School in Staten Island—was one of the first major live events John had performed at since the Beatles played Candlestick Park in 1966.

"Me best performance since Hamburg," an ecstatic John told me a few days afterwards. "It was like the old days. I felt the energy."

I was feeling pretty good myself as well, having just landed a new job. And not just any job, but a talk show program on KABC, sister station to KLOS, the one that had fired me for playing *Some Time in New York City*. Unlike, KLOS, KABC didn't broadcast music—it was all talk, all the time—which I guess made its station management feel better about bringing me aboard. After all, I'd never gotten in trouble for anything I'd *said* on the air, just for what I put on a turntable. Also, as it turned out, my firing may have ultimately enhanced my reputation as a broadcaster. I wouldn't go so far as to say it made me a cause célèbre, but it did give me a smidge of rebel cred, which KABC did their best to exploit.

For starters, they put my face on billboards around town. "Elliot Mintz, Communicator," the fourteen-foot-high ads announced. When I first spotted one, I was horrified. It wasn't just that the black-and-white photo they picked made me look twelve years old; that I could live with. Rather, I worried that any picture of me on a billboard would blow up the anonymity I so relished as a radio broadcaster. While I was happy more listeners were hearing my interviews, I was much less pleased with the idea that people might recognize my face.

But the job itself was a joy. I'd drive my old, jittery Jag to the familiar block-long broadcasting complex off La Cienega Boulevard that housed both radio stations, stroll into the lobby, and head down the hallway, just as I used to. But instead of turning left into KLOS's studios, I veered right into KABC's. And what a difference that turn made. KLOS was a legendary rock 'n' roll station, so its employees tended to be people on the cutting edge—or at least they had long hair and wore jeans. Most of those who toiled across the hall at KABC wore jackets and ties, had much shorter hair, and sometimes even carried briefcases. It was two totally different corporate cultures under one roof. But somehow, everybody got along. Indeed, some of my best friends in that building had crew cuts.

My new show was still predominantly an interview program, mostly focusing on musicians and other cultural icons. But because music wasn't played on KABC, I had to find other ways to keep listeners amused when I wasn't chatting with the likes of Norman Mailer and John Wayne. So I borrowed some techniques

from the great Steve Allen—one of my early broadcast idols—
and filled airtime with lighthearted phone schtick. I had my producer Barney drive around town and get the numbers for phone
booths at various locations—in LAX, at a bus station, outside a
strip club in Hollywood, by a gas station in Oxnard—and I'd
ring them just to see who answered.

Another running gag involved my perennial quest to track
down and interview the elusive Howard Hughes. If I got a tip on
the billionaire's whereabouts, I'd call whatever hotel he was ru-
mored to be ensconced in and try to bluff my way into getting
him on the line. "Just tell him it's Elliot," I'd say to the front desk.
"Howard's expecting my call."

Needless to say, it never worked.

Even more challenging than getting Hughes on the phone,
though, was getting John and Yoko *off* the phone. Since San Francisco, they were calling more than ever, and at all hours. That
was one of the reasons I had the hotline installed: the Lennons
were occupying my other lines so much, nobody else could get
through. Giving them their own number seemed like a prag-
matic way to keep my wires from getting crossed. As for mounting a flashing red light over my bed to wake me in the event of a
late-night John or Yoko call, well, that admittedly may have been
over-the-top. But by this point I had come to accept that being at
John and Yoko's beck and call was becoming my mission in life.

Why I accepted that mission, I couldn't tell you. I just did.

"Have you ever seen *The 700 Club*?" John asked during one
typical call.

108

"Um, I've checked it out," I responded with some hesitation.

"I've been watching it lately and I'm wondering what you think of it."

John watched a lot of TV—at one point, he imported an early-generation big-screen set from Japan that he kept at the foot of his bed, almost always turned on, although usually with the volume off—but I had a hard time imagining him watching Pat Robertson. Why in heaven's name would the guy who wrote such secular classics as "Imagine" and "God" find anything engaging about a Bible-waving evangelist on daytime television?

"He seems like a fundamentalist preacher with very conservative views," I said. "What do you think of The 700 Club?"

"Well," John answered, "I think the show could use a band and some music. But I've been paying attention to some of the things Robertson says about Jesus. Ya know, I hide behind a Buddhist façade when it suits me, but I was born a Christian. And when Robertson is quoting Jesus, it rings some old bells." He paused pensively. "I think you should watch the show tomorrow," he went on. "We should both watch. And talk about it afterwards, about how Robertson quotes Jesus."

"John, are you kidding?"

"Of course not! I'm bloody serious. Why the fuck would you think this is a joke?"

I promised to watch The 700 Club and call John afterwards.

The following day, I did indeed tune in to the program. I even took notes. And afterwards I dutifully called John so we could share our impressions.

"Oh," he said. "I didn't watch it. I fell asleep. We can try again another time."

John and religion was always a fascinating topic, and maybe one where I made my biggest misstep. John and I were talking about the song "God"; the song where he lists all the deities that he personally rejects, ranging from Jesus to the Beatles themselves. He asked me what I thought of it. I said, "It's a very powerful song, John, but if it were me, I wouldn't have personalized it. I would say to the audience, 'You may believe in Buddha, you may believe in Krishna' . . . going down the entire list . . . finally getting to the payoff of 'I just believe in me.' I think that would be a gutsier way to say it." He glared at me and said, "Fuck off." Looking back, I can't believe my sheer audacity—one of the greatest songwriters in history, and I told him how I thought he should have written the song. Even though I wasn't always a fan of John's saltier language, it was justified this time.

In any case, Robertson never came up in our phone calls again.

ONE frequent topic of discussion with John was Hollywood personalities. He was fascinated by movie stars, especially those of more classic vintage. I remember once telling him I was about to interview Mae West; he all but demanded I bring him back an autographed photo of the seminal cinematic sex symbol from the 1930s. West, who was in her eighties at the time, was happy to oblige. But she signed the photo, "To John Lemon."

He loved that picture. He kept it forever.

"If you could interview anyone in the world, who would it be?" he asked me during another call.

"Living or dead?" I responded.

"They're much easier to get when they're alive, aren't they?" he said.

I told him about my efforts to reach Howard Hughes on my radio show—how fascinated I was with the billionaire.

John was baffled at first. "Howard Hughes? Why Howard Hughes?"

"Do you know much about him?" I went on, eager to share my personal passion for Hughes-ography. "He's one of the richest men in the world and a total recluse. He hasn't been seen in public since 1952. He bought and sold TWA over the phone. He purchased seven hotels on the Vegas Strip without ever appearing in front of the gaming commission. He's been hiding out in hotels, putting aluminum foil on the windows to keep out the sun and prying eyes, never cutting his fingernails or toenails, wearing Kleenex boxes on his feet to keep out germs. He has bizarre diets where for months all he eats is ice cream. He has this one guy, his right-hand man—a former FBI agent named Robert Maheu—who carries out his instructions. Hughes writes them out on yellow pads of paper and sends them to Maheu. They've been doing it for twenty years. And yet Maheu has never actually met Hughes face to face . . ."

John listened to my Hughes tutorial with rapt attention. When I finished, he let out a belly laugh.

"That's fucking great!" he exclaimed. "Hughes doesn't want to deal with any of these wankers, so he told them all to sod off! He dropped out from everything to live his life without anybody asking any questions. I understand this bloke completely. I totally get the guy."

Years later, some would confuse John's bemused affection for Hughes with a desire to replicate his eccentric lifestyle—or would accuse Yoko of locking him away in Hughes-like exile. In some circles, it became something of a Lennon trope, John as the lunatic loner. But it wasn't remotely true. The fact is, John's so-called Hughes obsession began and ended as a joke.

ANOTHER regular conversational pit stop during our calls was the guests I was interviewing on my radio show on any given week, especially if they were rock stars. Inevitably, John would have some spirited opinions to share about his competition. One time, for instance, I casually mentioned an upcoming booking with Mick Jagger.

"Why are you interviewing *him*?" John asked.

The truth was, I was interviewing Jagger because he was holding a concert in L.A. to raise money for victims of an earthquake in Nicaragua. (His wife, Bianca, was Nicaraguan.) But for some reason I foolishly blurted out, "Because the Rolling Stones are probably the greatest live touring band in the world."

"Isn't that what they used to say about us?" John coolly replied.

"But the Beatles aren't touring anymore," I said, stepping on a landmine. "The Beatles as a group don't exist anymore. And the Rolling Stones are as important a presence as anybody in rock 'n' roll."

"The Rolling Stones followed us!" John shouted. "Just look at the albums! Their *Satanic* gobbledygook came right after *Sgt. Pepper*. We were there first. The only difference is that we got labeled as the mop tops and they were put out there as revolutionaries. Look, Ellie," he went on, "I spent a lot of time with Mick. We palled around in London. We go way back. But the Beatles were the revolutionaries, not the Rolling Pebbles!"

John and I didn't often talk about the Beatles, largely because it was the one subject other people, particularly in the media, were always asking him about. He'd been answering questions about the group's history for so long, rehashing its mythology over and over again, that by now the subject bored the hell out of him. "It was like a marriage," he once told me. "I enjoyed the beginning more than I enjoyed the end, when we were doing those live shows and nobody could hear the music over the screaming. Everyone else was having a good time yelling and shouting, but we were suffering up there. We were just going through the motions. We couldn't hear our own selves singing."

In other words, John had moved on from the Beatles, even if the rest of the world had not.

Still, from time to time, the topic inevitably reared its head, particularly when one of his old bandmates released a new solo album. John had complicated, mercurial feelings about his fellow

Beatles, to put it mildly, and it was impossible to predict at any given moment what he might say about any of them. He loved Paul like a brother, of course, but sometimes hated him like a brother, too. The sibling rivalry between them ran soul-deep, especially whenever Paul and his new band, Wings, chalked up another hit on the charts. John was less jealous of George, but then, they'd never been as close, particularly after George convinced the Beatles to take that 1968 sojourn to India to study Transcendental Meditation with Maharishi Mahesh Yogi, who John ultimately concluded was a phony. Of them all, only Ringo remained unscathed by John's grudges. I can't recall John ever uttering a negative word about the drummer. But everybody always loved Ringo.

And yet, paradoxically, John could also be fiercely defensive about his old band. Ironically, he often complained that the Beatles, the single most successful and influential group in the history of rock music, weren't taken seriously enough. He resented the cute, cuddly image the "Fab Four" had initially been saddled with—ever since appearing on *The Ed Sullivan Show* in those matching Chesterfield suits—while other, scruffier troubadours of the era, like Mick Jagger, were allotted much cooler, iconoclastic labels, like "revolutionaries."

Which is why, as I learned early in our relationship, one was well-advised to tread lightly around the subject of a certain other man whom many considered to be the greatest living lyricist. The mere mention of Bob Dylan's name during one of our phone calls could uncork a volcano of roiling resentments and pent-up jealousies—not to mention one of John's startlingly accurate impersonations. (John could be a fierce mimic, particularly of Dylan.)

"Everybody looks on him as if he's some kind of genius," John would grumble. "And everybody remembers the Beatles for 'I Want to Hold Your Hand.' But I'm just as good a songwriter as Dylan! My songs are very simple, very direct. There's poetry in them, but it's working-class rock 'n' roll poetry. That's what I do: I make rock music! I don't know what to call what *he* makes!"

In some ways, the Beatles and Dylan—two cultural forces that shaped the zeitgeist of the 1960s more than any other musicians—traveled parallel paths. They both burst onto the scene at nearly the exact same moment: "I Want to Hold Your Hand" and Dylan's "Blowin' in the Wind" were released within months of each other in 1963. In fact, John and his bandmates met Dylan not long afterwards: in 1964, when the Beatles played Forest Hills Tennis Stadium in New York, Dylan dropped by their rooms at the Delmonico Hotel for what turned out to be a pivot point in music history. It was the first time any of the Beatles smoked pot. According to those who were there, Dylan rolled a joint and handed it to John, who immediately gave it to Ringo (his "royal taster," John supposedly joked). Ringo, unschooled in the decorum of joint sharing, smoked the entire doobie himself. Another was rolled, and when John finally inhaled, it was love at first toke. All the Beatles were instantly smitten.

"We were smoking marijuana for breakfast," John once confessed. "Nobody could communicate with us: we were just glazed eyes, giggling all the time."

But, of course, over the ensuing years the Beatles and Dylan would veer off into very different creative forks, approaching music from diametrically opposite directions. Some of the Beatles—especially George—found Dylan's cerebral, genre-bending sonic sonnets inspiring, and Dylan clearly pushed the Beatles to experiment, starting on 1966's *Revolver*, where the band first began to wander into psychedelic pastures (and where George first picked up a sitar). John, too, found some of Dylan's music inventive; Paul once even suggested that John tried to sing like Dylan on "You've Got to Hide Your Love Away." But for John, Dylan worship was also a source of massive frustration. After all, John was the greatest songwriter of his generation—at least according to John. Dylan should have been inspired by the Beatles, not the other way around.

What really stuck in John's craw, though, was when Dylan announced he'd become a born-again Christian. I remember talking to John on the phone after Dylan's appearance on *Saturday Night Live* in the late 1970s, when he showed up at Studio 8H wearing a mostly white outfit and sang his new hit single, "Gotta Serve Somebody."

"The guy's just making a fool out of himself," John scoffed. "He looks like a preacher and he's singing gibberish!"

"He does strike a resonant chord with so many people," I said, foolishly attempting to defend Dylan. (As it happened, I was a huge fan.)

"So many?" John sneered back at me. "The Beatles probably outsold him by a hundred million!"

"You know," I went on, pushing my luck, "I think that a lot of your disdain for him comes out of jealousy."

"Fuck off," John said. "You think I'm jealous of Dylan?"

"I don't think you're jealous of his songwriting abilities," I continued. "I think you're jealous of the way people perceive him. You hate that people think he's this great poet, because they perceive his music to be more surreal and dreamlike than the Beatles'."

"Listen to 'Walrus,'" John said.

I tried a different track. "His style and performance are what's appealing to people," I said. "People like his voice. *I* like his voice."

"You're hung up on style," he said. "What I create is music. Look, I loved him when he put out 'Subterranean Homesick Blues,' with those lyrics about 'Don't follow leaders / Watch the parkin' meters.' Everything else about the so-called wandering poet is irrelevant to me."

We would go back and forth like this for years.

Of course, my conversations with John were only part of what kept my ear glued to the hotline in my Laurel Canyon house. I spent just as many hours talking to Yoko, although her calls tended to be considerably less confrontational and gossipy. In part, that's because Yoko was a less confrontational person who had much less interest in the comings and goings of celebrities. But it was also because she was the boss behind her and John's businesses. She handled the staffing, talked to the lawyers, approved the dealmaking, and dealt with the moneymen. She didn't have time for much else. When she set off the flashing red light on my bedroom ceiling with a call at four or five in the morning, she usually got right down to what was important. And what was important to Yoko was numbers—and not always the ones with dollar signs in front of them.

Yoko's world turned on numerology, astrology, tarot cards, and other psychic belief systems. She had a coterie of spiritual advisors and they vetted virtually every decision Yoko made, from whom to do business with to what flight to take when they were traveling. (Indeed, in this regard, she was advised by no less an authority than Takashi Yoshikawa, aka Mr. K, an expert in katatagae, an ancient Japanese belief system in which the directions taken during a journey possess important meaning and value.) When I asked about inviting Louise to dine with us in Sausalito, for instance, Yoko's only comment was that she had been "checked." I knew that meant at least one of Yoko's advisors had deemed Louise an acceptable dinner companion.

I was not completely unfamiliar with astrology—I'd undergone a few readings myself—but I was a little concerned that Yoko was basing so many critical (and not-so-critical) life decisions on messages from the psychic ether. John seemed perfectly fine with it because he had absolute faith in his wife. If she believed something, he believed it, even if he didn't. To me, though, it seemed risky, and I pressed Yoko about it, asking her why she put so much trust in the paranormal.

"It is very important while seeking truth to get out of the rational mind," she answered patiently. "As long as you let your brain come to conclusions, it can be influenced by your mood, the time of day, what you've eaten, your emotions. It's only when you remove yourself from all that, that's when people see clearest."

The downside of numerology, however, was that it required a lot of, well, numbers—like the birth dates of the people Yoko wanted to have "checked out." And this, unfortunately for me, became the subject of many of my middle-of-the-night hotline calls with her.

"Elliot, we are aware that you know everybody in Hollywood," she began one of them.

"I think that might be an exaggeration," I responded.

"There is this person in Los Angeles that we might be doing business with," she went on, giving me the person's name. "I need you to get some information on him before we proceed with the business."

"You mean a background check?" I asked. "Like arrest records and things like that?"

"No," Yoko said. "I need the year this person was born."

"Uh-huh," I said.

"Also, it would be helpful if you could find the exact time this person was born and where the birth occurred."

"Uh-huh," I said again.

"Do you think you can get this information, Elliot? Will you help us?"

"Well," I said, "the only thing I can think of is hiring a private investigator I know; he might be able to dig up those sorts of things. Let me give him a try."

A few hours later, when the sun came up, I gave my PI friend a call. After I told him what I was looking for—never mentioning Yoko, of course—he gave me a discourse on various investigative techniques, including one called "dumpster diving." If he could find an address for the person in question, he'd send his team to his house and confiscate his garbage, which technically became public once it was in a trash can on the street. "You'd be surprised at how much information you can learn about someone from their garbage," he said. "What prescriptions they took, what magazines they read, old pay stubs and bills. That might give us a trail to his birth date." He would check with a source at the Department of Water and Power and see if they had an address. He'd get back to me shortly.

No sooner had I hung up the phone with the PI than the hotline rang again. It was Yoko.

"Did you get the information yet?" she whispered. "Did you get his birth date?"

"Yoko, you only asked me for it three hours ago. It's going to take time."

"I don't have time, Elliot," she said, annoyed. "Can't you understand that?"

Luckily for Yoko—although not so much for me—the PI hit pay dirt. Within a day, he had procured enough numbers for Yoko's staff astrologers to complete an analysis. She was so impressed with the results that she started calling me several times a month with similar birth date inquiries. Suddenly, I was her clearinghouse for all her dumpster-diving needs.

I can't tell you how much I disliked those requests.

Before too long, I was spending more time on the phone with John and Yoko than I was on the radio. In a very real sense, my friendship with them had become my primary occupation, although it was hardly a lucrative gig. Even though I ended up picking up some of the bills for the private investigator—at $250 a pop—I could seldom bring myself to ask them to pay me back. I knew people were constantly looking for ways to get money from them, sending them invoices for anything they could think of, trying to take advantage of their wealth and financial generosity. The last thing I wanted was to be seen as one of those opportunists.

But the good news was that I was being paid well by KABC and was thoroughly enjoying my new job. In fact, there were moments during my show when I felt connected to the city and my listeners in ways I'd seldom felt before. Indeed, one of the more gratifying experiences I ever had on the air took place around this time, during one of those segments when I dialed a random pay phone to see who might pick up. On this particular occasion, I called a booth at a bus station in Hollywood.

After a few rings, a woman's voice said, "Hello?"

"Hello! My name is Elliot Mintz. I'm calling from KABC Radio. You're on the air. Who am I speaking with?"

She hesitated and then gave me her first name.

"And how are you doing tonight? Have you just arrived in Los Angeles?"

"No, mister," she said wearily. "I'm on my way out. I'm going home."

"Why?" I asked. "Why are you leaving?"

"Oh, you know, I came here with my wishes and dreams, and everything just fell apart. Nothing lasted. Not the job, not the husband. Nothing. So I just want to go home and be with Mama."

"I'm so sorry to hear that," I said.

"If I don't go home, I'll be sleeping on the streets."

"What kind of work were you doing in L.A.?"

"Oh, just some housekeeping and chores. Things like that. I'm a hard worker. Always do my best. But my bus will be here in forty minutes."

I could hear such heaviness in her ragged voice, such genuine sorrow, it all but broke my heart. But then I got an idea.

"Can you just stick with us here on the phone for five minutes? I'm gonna put you on hold for a bit, but don't go away, okay?"

"I got nothing else to do, mister."

I kept the mic open and stayed on the air while I put her on hold.

"Look," I said to my listeners, "if anybody out there needs a housekeeper, or has some other work for this woman, or just wants to give her a second chance, call the station right now. Let's see if we can help her out." I gave them a direct number to Barney behind the glass wall and crossed my fingers.

Within seconds, Barney's phone lit up. A dozen people had called in. I put the woman at the bus station back on the air.

"Listen," I said, "you might not believe this, but there are a number of people in Los Angeles who were listening to you on the radio, and they want to talk to you about offering you a job."

"Is this some kind of joke? Because too many people have joked with me in this city."

"No, it's no joke at all. My producer is going to give you their numbers, off the air, and you can call them right now from your phone booth."

She took a second to process what was happening. Then, her voice quivering, she whispered "Thank you" into the phone.

"I don't know where this is going," I told my listeners after I transferred the woman to Barney's line. "You're hearing all this in real time. After tonight, we may never learn what happened with this woman at the bus station. But thanks for tuning in. And to all the people who called in to help her out, thank you for caring."

"This is Elliot Mintz on KABC," I said, feeling better about the world than I had in ages. "We'll be right back."

SEVEN

Los Angeles and New York, 1972 to 1973

One of the best parts of being a radio show host was that I got to meet many of the people I'd grown up admiring and even glorifying.

It was also one of the worst parts of the job.

Nobody in real life is ever as impressive as they are up on a screen, on a stage, or in a concert hall. Art tends to glamorize the artist, sets them apart, imbues them with what fans mistake as superhuman powers. In truth, they're just people, as flawed and fallible and, ultimately, disappointing as the rest of us wayward souls. Not even John Wayne—one of my early childhood fixations—could live up to my outsized expectations for him. When I sat down to interview the Duke on my show not long before he died at seventy-two from stomach cancer, he was simply a tired old man with sandbag eyes and an all-too-obvious hair-piece pasted to his forehead.

Not that John and Yoko were disappointments: in many ways, they were as impressive in person as they were on vinyl or video.

As public figures in the late '60s and early '70s, I was drawn to them as much for their political activism as their art. I agreed with their outspoken opposition to the war in Vietnam. I thought their bed-ins for peace were brilliant. In television appearances, they always came across as witty and articulate; I found them exemplary spokespeople for the counterculture. Most of all, though, I was charmed by how sincere they seemed. They appeared to have an unshakable, almost childlike faith in the prospect of a better world. All that was required for human-kind to live together in harmony and love, they believed, was for enough people to imagine it was possible. They even rented a billboard in Times Square—around Christmas of 1969, at the height of the slaughter in Southeast Asia—spelling out their message in big block letters. "WAR IS OVER!" it said. "If you want it."

Yes, I suppose you could say they were dreamers, and, no, they were not the only ones. I personally found their idealism infectious and inspiring, and so did millions of others. Still, as I got to know John and Yoko as flesh-and-blood friends—or, in those days, more often as incorporeal voices on the phone—I began to see their flawed human sides as well.

Yoko, for one, was even more airy and ethereal in private

than she was in the media. She could be a fountain of apho-risms, dispensing endless nuggets of Zen-like philosophy. Her haiku-esque homilies on manifesting one's desires or the wisdom of the nonrational mind could be a bit much for some people. There were moments, I confess, when even I was a bit baffled by it all. Except then she would say or do something that would ab-solutely convince me that she was connected to some higher plane.

"You had a dream two nights ago, didn't you?" she asked me out of the blue during one particularly long phone call. "It was about your mother, wasn't it?"

I was stunned. I had indeed had a dream about my mother, one that I was sure I hadn't told a soul about. Or at least at the time I was pretty sure I hadn't.

"You were arguing with her about your childhood stut-ter, yes?"

I gripped the hotline as tightly as if I were strangling it. How could she possibly know? My mother and I were arguing about my stutter in my dream, and when I woke up it left me feeling insecure and inadequate.

"But you speak beautifully now, Elliot," Yoko went on. "Peo-ple pay you to speak on the radio. You won the struggle with your stutter because you imagined you could change. Your stut-ter is gone because you wanted it gone."

As John had told me in Ojai, Yoko saw things other people didn't. I came to conclude that he was right.

John, meanwhile, was every bit as charming, funny, and in-telligent as he came across in public. But I gradually discovered he was far from perfect. For starters, for a guy who aspired to be a world-shaking peacemaker—a thought leader on par with Mahatma Gandhi, Martin Luther King Jr., and Nelson Mandela—he was surprisingly uninformed about historic figures like, well, Gandhi, King, and Mandela. John was a voracious consumer of books—he devoured George Orwell, Lewis Carroll, Jonathan Swift, Dylan Thomas, James Thurber, Oscar Wilde, Edgar Allan Poe, James Joyce, and scores of other classic and contemporary authors—but there were still some noticeable gaps in his reading, chapters he skipped over. Although he admired Gandhi and the others as models of nonviolence, he knew relatively little about their biographies or their movements.

He also had some Luddite-like notions about science, particularly medicine, extending well beyond his annoyance at "daddy doctors" for not letting him perform his own weight-loss injections. Even though John had smoked, ingested, or snorted just about every illegal recreational drug he could get his hands on, he was weirdly suspicious of the ones that were properly prescribed and proven efficacious. He was, in fact, one of the original anti-vaxxers. After Sean's birth, he would try everything he could to keep his son away from the needle. (Eventually, Sean did get vaccinated.)

They were paradoxes, John and Yoko, filled to the brim with internal contradictions. That was the main thing I learned about them during those early years of our friendship. On the one hand, they could be incredibly sensitive, honest, provocative, caring, creative, generous, and wise. On the other, they could be self-centered, desperate, vain, petty, and annoying. In John's case, also shockingly cruel—even to Yoko.

An example . . .

Early one morning in November 1972, the red light over my bed started blinking. I picked up the hotline.

"Ellie, I fucked up" were the first words out of John's mouth.

"Why?" I groggily asked. "What did you do?"

"We were at this party last night," he said, "and I got loaded. And there was a girl . . ."

I sat up in bed.

The party was at Jerry Rubin's Greenwich Village apartment. A small crowd of well-connected peaceniks had gathered to watch the presidential election returns on television, hoping against hope that George McGovern would somehow pull off a political miracle. But as the vote totals started piling up and it became clear that Richard Nixon would win reelection by a landslide, the mood grew bleaker and the crowd began drinking more heavily.

Alcohol was not John's friend. While pot relaxed and inspired him, drinking tended to make him mean-spirited and reckless, unleashing bitter demons. And on this occasion, John's evil inner gremlins truly outdid themselves.

I got some of the specifics from a hungover John during his morning-after call. A devastated Yoko would later fill in even more embarrassing details. But the upshot was that John had indeed hit it off with some girl at the party and had slipped into a bedroom with her, where they proceeded to have such loud, raucous sex that everyone sitting around the TV in Jerry Rubin's living room—including Yoko—could clearly hear them going at it.

At one point during the noisy indiscretion, a well-meaning party guest put a record on the turntable—Bob Dylan's eleven-minute ballad "Sad Eyed Lady of the Lowlands"—and played it at high volume, trying to drown out the rhythmic pounding. But not even Dylan's inimitable singing could distract from the racket John and his hookup were making in the bedroom on the other side of what must have been a paper-thin wall. Throughout it all, Yoko sat on the sofa in stunned, mortified silence as other guests began awkwardly getting up to leave—until they realized that their coats were in the bedroom where John was having sex.

I don't know how long it lasted—I wasn't there, thank God; I was 2,500 miles away in Laurel Canyon—but I imagine that Rubin's apartment cleared out the instant John and the woman emerged from the bedroom and people could finally reclaim their garments. I'm certain John and Yoko made a speedy exit, sharing what must have been a frosty walk or cab ride home to their own apartment, at that time on Bank Street in the Village. Whatever they said to each other later that night, I suspect the conversation was not a pleasant one.

"I slept on the sofa," John told me over the phone, sounding defeated and embarrassed—although, frankly, not quite as contrite as I thought his situation warranted. More than anything, he seemed annoyed with himself for committing what he clearly believed was a stupid but relatively petty transgression.

"Things like that happen," he said, way too matter-of-factly for my taste. "A bloke cheats on his wife . . . If I weren't famous, nobody would care."

Yoko, unsurprisingly, felt differently.

"Are you okay?" I gently asked her when I phoned to check in on her a few hours later.

"There is no answer to that question," she said shakily.

"Do you think you'll ever be able to forgive him?"

"I can forgive him," she said. "But I don't know if I can ever forget what happened. I don't know if it will ever be the same."

She sounded so weak and humiliated, it broke my heart. As soon as we hung up the phone—it was a short conversation—I found myself contemplating what had once been unthinkable. For the first time since I'd met them, I considered the very real possibility that they might break up. I tried to imagine a world in which John and Yoko were no longer together. I couldn't do it. To me, they were a magical couple. They defined each other, amplified one another's brilliance, fit so perfectly that they seemed to have been mated by the stars. How could they not be together?

Also, to be completely honest, I was concerned about my own fate. I wondered whether my friendships with them could survive a split. Who would get custody of me? How could I possibly remain friends with just one of them? Or would I end up being abandoned by them both?

After a few weeks of cooling down, though—during which Yoko wrote and recorded "Death of Samantha," her bluesy ode to burying one's pain for the sake of outward appearances—the crisis *seemed* to abate. Over the coming months, they *appeared* to go back to their lives, making every effort to put the incident behind them, or at least paper it over as best they could. And for a while it worked. Yoko tried to forgive, even if she ultimately couldn't. And John—perhaps finally feeling an appropriate level of guilt—had never been a more doting husband.

Three months after Jerry Rubin's party, in February of 1973, the Lennons flew to Los Angeles to attend a party of my own. It was my twenty-eighth birthday, and I decided to host a soiree for myself at my Laurel Canyon home. I invited my neighbors— Harry Nilsson, Alice Cooper, Micky Dolenz—and a few others, including Louise, who drove down from Mill Valley to attend, as well as John and Yoko, who I knew were heading to L.A. to publicize Yoko's newly released album, *Approximately Infinite Universe*. It was, in a way, a coming-out party: the first time I would introduce my old Laurel Canyon buddies to my new, up-until-then-secret friends, the ones who'd been mysteriously occupying so much of my time on the telephone.

I was a little nervous about it beforehand, worrying about how John and Yoko would feel about going public with our relationship, whether they'd play nice with the other people in my life. I thought about that awkward dinner with Louise in Sausalito and hoped this wouldn't be a repeat. But it couldn't have gone better. Within moments of arriving, John and Yoko were mingling like they'd lived in the Canyon all their lives. The two of them, I noticed, didn't spend a whole lot of time with each other—mostly they socialized separately—but they both seemed in good spirits. Indeed, at the end of the night, John even broke into a spontaneous jam session with several of my other musician friends.

It was a huge relief. From then on, I no longer had to hide what was quickly becoming the most important relationship in my life.

A few days later, I interviewed Yoko on my radio show. As it happened, it was now *her* birthday—she was born February 18; I was born the sixteenth—so I decided to make it a special occasion. Unlike my first interview with Yoko, which had been conducted by phone, we would do this one in person at KABC. John insisted on coming to the studio as well, to cheer Yoko on, even though he worried his presence might distract from his wife's moment in the spotlight. He was right to be concerned. Sure enough, as I escorted them through the building, heads popped out of office doorways to catch a glimpse of the former Beatle as he ambled down KABC's hallways. By the time we settled in front of the mic, there was a small crowd of looky-loos peering at him through one of the studio's glass walls.

The attention clearly put John off: he was determined to give Yoko her due. So, not only did he remain completely silent during her forty-five-minute interview—no easy task for such a natural-born talker—he made himself disappear, hiding under the studio table so that he no longer drew any attention. It was awkward, for sure, and it couldn't have been a comfortable fit for John, but it struck me as being as chivalrous a gesture as anything Sir Walter Raleigh ever did with a cloak and a puddle.

Still, as gallant as John was, and as cheerful as Yoko sounded during her radio interview, it was hard not to notice the chill that had settled between them.

Afterwards, we grabbed a late-night dinner at a sushi restaurant on La Cienega Boulevard near the studio. While their appetites had improved since their detoxing road trip to San Francisco, the mood at our table was palpably less festive than it had been in the Dragon Wagon. There was no hand-holding between John and Yoko. No soft kisses to each other's foreheads. Barely any eye contact at all. They were cordial towards one another—John was flawlessly attentive—but the air around them was noticeably nippy.

"Would you like to go anywhere else tonight, Mother?" John asked her as we finished our green tea at the end of the meal."

"No, I'm tired," she said without so much as glancing at her husband. "Elliot, would you mind driving us back to our hotel?"

I looked at John. From the uneasiness in his expression, I could tell their marriage was still in trouble. In fact, it was hanging by a thread.

To be fair, there was more going on here than marital stress. One of the downsides of Nixon's reelection—aside from the still-raging war in Vietnam, the looming Watergate scandal, and a slew of other crimes and misdemeanors—was that the White House could spend another four years breathing down John's neck.

The threat of deportation was clearly weighing heavily on the Lennons, and with good reason. Although the FBI's surveillance efforts hadn't yielded any actionable evidence, Nixon's operatives had cooked up a new scheme to boot John back to England: they would use a minor 1968 marijuana infraction in London, when John was fined 150 pounds for possession of some hashish (later revealed to have been planted by police), as a pretext to expel him from the United States. Nixon's underlings wasted little time in executing the plan. In March 1973, a month after my birthday party in Laurel Canyon, John was served with a deportation order in New York.

John felt strongly about staying in New York—he had come to love America. He felt free here, removed from the chaos of life in the UK. He felt like anywhere he went in Great Britain, he and Yoko would be mobbed. That was true in some parts of the United States as well, as I had witnessed during our trip to San Francisco. New Yorkers, though, were more indifferent about celebrities—they'd seen them come and seen them go—so for the most part, John was able to live something approximating a normal life in Manhattan.

He also appreciated America's much looser class system. Of course, there was nothing close to class equality in the United States, but there was certainly more social mobility here than in his homeland. America was at least a few inches closer to John's ideal of a classless society. Here, he felt, he really could be a "working class hero," as he titled one of his songs.

So he was determined to stay in the States and would fight deportation, his case wending through the labyrinth of the U.S. legal system. Ultimately, he'd be victorious. John would officially become a permanent resident of the United States a few years later, in 1976.

Still, at the time, in the spring of '73, John's future in America—a country he had come to love as his own—was uncertain. Equally uncertain were his prospects with Yoko, who was obviously still processing her husband's election-night betrayal, weighing whether to stay in the marriage. For all either John or Yoko knew, they were on the precipice of losing everything that meant anything to them: their adopted homeland, their musical partnership, the life they had built together in New York.

Being John and Yoko, paradigms of paradoxes, they responded to this profound moment of doubt and turmoil by doubling down on each other. They chose to roll the cosmic dice with a spectacular gesture of faith and hope in the staying power of their love.

They bought an apartment in the Dakota.

EIGHT

New York and Los Angeles, 1973

t's apartment number 72," Yoko excitedly announced when she called to tell me about the Dakota purchase. "Do you see the significance, Elliot? Do you understand what that number means?"

It took a little math tutoring, but Yoko explained exactly what that number meant, at least to her and John. When you added seven and two, you got nine. And nine was a hugely significant numeral to the Lennons, a magic integer that seemed to mysteriously recur throughout John's life. Yoko would rattle off the number's many repeated appearances: John was born on the ninth of October. She was born on the eighteenth of February (one plus eight). The first home he lived in—his grandfather's house—was at 9 Newcastle Road. Paul McCartney's last name has nine letters. The Beatles' first appearance at the Cavern Club was on the ninth of February 1961. Their first appearance on *Ed Sullivan* was on February 9, 1964. The band broke up in 1969, after nine years of making music together.

Some would say all the above was merely coincidence. John and Yoko believed otherwise.

Numerological portents aside, I was thrilled the Lennons were starting afresh in a new home on the Upper West Side, even if I was somewhat mystified as to why they chose this particular neighborhood. Moving from Greenwich Village to the Dakota was almost like decamping to an entirely different city, or even country, maybe even planet. Bank Street was a quaint tree-lined lane filled with tidy brick town houses; the Dakota, in contrast, was a Gilded Age grande dame of an edifice with a sandstone petticoat that stretched a city block. The Village was populated with hippies and artists and other free spirits; the Dakota's tenants were old-money pillars of the establishment, with the occasional smattering of vintage Hollywood and Broadway royalty, like Lauren Bacall and Jason Robards. Other residents included Leonard Bernstein, Rudolf Nureyev, Rex Reed, and, at one point, Boris Karloff. Interesting neighbors, to be sure, but not exactly John and Yoko's milieu.

"Aren't you worried it'll be too stuffy for you?" I asked John. "Will the people who live there even know who you are?"

"I don't want them to know who we are!" he said with a laugh. "I don't want to know who *they* are! We just want to be left alone. When can you come see it? Can you get here tomorrow?"

While it wasn't unusual in those days for me to jet to New

York on a moment's notice—especially when John or Yoko asked me—this time I could not get there so quickly. At that point, my own life in L.A. had taken a surreal turn, becoming much busier and far more complicated. Like a character out of a Kafka novel, I had recently undergone a strange and unexpected metamorphosis. Much to my horror, I awoke one day to discover that I had been transformed into a TV personality.

KABC Radio was affiliated with KABC TV, and somebody in the "Big Room" of the network brass got the bright idea to make me the "entertainment correspondent" for the 11:00 p.m. local TV news. The thinking, I guess, was that since I was already interviewing celebrities for my radio show, it would be easy—and inexpensive—to send a camera crew along with me to tape a few minutes of conversation for TV segments.

In practice, it was not nearly so simple. For one thing, while my radio discourses could stretch on for an hour or more, TV spots required a level of conversational brevity I was not used to. I had to learn to get in and out of an interview in two or three minutes. For another, television is a visual medium, which meant I had to put much more thought and effort into where my interviews would take place. One of my first on-camera segments for *Eyewitness News*, for instance, was with my old neighbor Alice Cooper, who had undergone a metamorphosis of his own, from humble Laurel Canyon minstrel to an enormously successful shock rock performer infamous for such stage stunts as impaling baby doll heads on spikes and strapping himself into an electric chair.

I ended up doing an on-camera interview with Alice at a golf course. Much to my surprise, it turned out he loved nothing more than hitting the links in his downtime.

Another complication: my radio show ended at 10:00 p.m., just an hour before the TV news went on the air. I had to dash from the studio on La Cienega up to East Hollywood, where the TV station was located, sit in a makeup chair while my face got Pan-Caked, and be camera-ready in time to shoot the live bumper that introduced whatever taped interview we had coming up. It was all incredibly, exhaustingly frantic.

But my biggest problem with being on TV was . . . being on TV. I had dabbled with video a few years earlier, hosting a super-low-budget UHF show called *Headshop*, on which I interviewed folks like Moe Howard of the Three Stooges (as well as a then completely unknown young piano player named Billy Joel). But the number of people tuning in to that tiny production airing on the remote outskirts of the dial—channel 52—could be counted on fingers and toes. KABC's local news program was broadcast on real VHS television—channel 7—reaching hundreds of thousands of viewers. Being on that show, I worried, could give me a far more recognizable face than I ever wanted to have.

"I wouldn't worry about it, Elliot," David Cassidy said with an eye roll when I told him my fears of losing my anonymity. "It's a local news show. I don't think we're talking about a crowd-control situation here."

David was correct, of course: I never did find myself scampering through train stations, Beatles-like, with hordes of fans chasing after me as "A Hard Day's Night" blared in the background. Occasionally, I might be at Canter's Deli, enjoying a bowl of matzo ball soup, when a viewer would shyly approach to tell me they enjoyed an interview I'd done on the news, but that was the extent of the privacy invasion. Besides, I was stuck with the gig; had I turned it down, my overlords at KABC could have easily replaced me—not just on TV but also on the radio. So I shrugged my shoulders and made the best of it, learning to smile graciously whenever I found myself being complimented by a stranger.

To be honest, a lot of this time frame is a little fuzzy. I like to think I have an excellent memory—borderline photographic— which is why I'm confident that the stories I'm putting down on these pages align with objective truth (to the degree that such a thing exists). But this particular period was so hectic and frenzied, a wild whirl of tapings and deadlines and mad dashes to interviews all over the city, that it tends to blend in my mind into a kaleidoscopic vision of blurry faces, names, and events.

However, I do recall with vivid clarity my first visit to John and Yoko's new apartment. After John's invitation, it took about a week for me to make space in my radio and TV schedule to fly east. I headed straight to the Dakota from JFK Airport, not bothering to stop off at the Plaza Hotel, where I usually stayed while in town. After the cab dropped me at the building's entrance on Seventy-Second Street, I stood for a moment on the sidewalk with my suitcase by my side, feeling like *The Great Gatsby*'s Nick Carraway arriving at West Egg for the first time, awed by the shoreline of this magnificent construction. The Dakota struck me as one of the most eerily beautiful—and oddly daunting—structures in all of New York City.

The main entrance was an archway—twenty feet tall, sixteen feet wide, big enough so that horse-drawn carriages could enter to drop off or pick up passengers—with heavy cast-iron gates that had to be manually operated by the doorman, who stood sentry in a booth. Back when it was first opened in 1884, it was the only building in the otherwise undeveloped wilderness of the Upper West Side, which was supposedly why its owner named it the Dakota. Well before 1973, of course, Manhattan had sprung up all around it, crowding the old pile with noisy younger neighbors, turning West Seventy-Second Street into a major spoke in the urban wheel of New York. Nevertheless, the Dakota still had the aura of a lone fortress standing guard on the edge of the frontier.

John and Yoko greeted me in the vaulted vestibule on the other side of the archway, all smiles and eager to begin our tour, which started not with their new apartment on the seventh floor but with a unit they had also purchased on the ground floor, which they were in the process of converting into office space. This, they excitedly explained, would be the new headquarters for Studio One, the business entity behind all of John and Yoko's creative enterprises. A few workmen were installing a floor-to-ceiling wall of file cabinets in its main room, and there were boxes and crates stacked in every corner, along with typewriters and mountains of other unpacked equipment.

Tellingly, John did not have an office in Studio One, but Yoko did. It was still taking shape, but the minute she opened its door, I could tell this was going to be the power center of the operation, the throne room of the Lennon empire (complete with its own private bathroom). There was an enormous antique Egyptian revival desk with hieroglyphics carved into its polished wood; a chaise longue covered in white fur; a fireplace; floor-to-ceiling darkened mirrors on one of the walls; a painted sky on the ceiling; and expensive-looking art deco lamps in the corner.

When they were done showing off Studio One, John and Yoko led me to the Dakota's elevator—said to be one of the first installed in the city—and we were hoisted up to the seventh floor, to the main attraction.

I'd visited some impressive homes in Los Angeles, from moguls' mansions to movie stars' penthouses, but nothing quite so striking as John and Yoko's new apartment. It was nearly 5,000 square feet, with dazzling high ceilings and massive windows offering eye-popping views of Central Park. It wasn't fully decorated yet, but it was much further along than the downstairs offices. Its expansive living room certainly seemed like a completed work—virtually everything in it, from the plush carpeting to the enormous wraparound sofa to the never-used fireplace to the grand Steinway piano (the one that appeared in John and Yoko's *Imagine* video), was as white as Japanese snowbells. The room even acquired a literal label: there was a gold plaque at its entrance identifying it officially as "The White Room."

Their aesthetic was minimalistic Shibui, with every surface

ruthlessly, if tastefully, stripped of ornamentation. There were no tchotchkes cluttering any shelves, no figurines adorning glass cabinets, not even many paintings on the walls.

In fact, other than the piano and one or two other pieces (like the eighteenth-century writing desk that once belonged to Scottish poet Robert Burns), there was only one highly conspicuous work of art in the White Room: a plexiglass case on a white pedestal maybe five feet long. Inside the case was a 3,000-year-old sarcophagus. John and Yoko had scored the very last mummy allowed out of Egypt before the Egyptian government put a ban on exporting their national antiquities.

"You should x-ray it and see what's inside," I suggested. "There might be something of great value, like precious jewels."

"I don't care what's inside," Yoko responded matter-of-factly. "The great value is the magic of the mummy itself."

I didn't realize it then, of course, but as John and Yoko led me through their new apartment—its large, comfortable kitchen where we would share so many meals over the coming years; the master bedroom where I would spend so many happy hours in a white wicker chair, talking with them late into the night—I was receiving a tour of my own future. It was my first glimpse of a world that would eventually become as familiar to me as my own much more modest house in Laurel Canyon, almost as if John and Yoko were welcoming *me* home.

Another thing I clearly remember about that long afternoon at the Dakota was how enthusiastic both John and Yoko seemed about the life they were building together in this marvelous new nest. They were full of plans for the place. John giddily described the "entertainment center" he wanted to construct in a nook off the kitchen. Yoko, ever the artist, chattered about the endless design ideas she had for the space. Their excitement was so infectious, it was all too easy to forget about the pain and stress—and, for Yoko, the humiliation—they'd been dealing with over the past several months, ever since the now never-spoken-of incident at Jerry Rubin's party.

As I was flying back to Los Angeles a few days later, I managed to convince myself that the worst was over for John and Yoko. They had worked through their issues. They had put the past behind them. John had learned his lesson and Yoko had managed to forgive, if not forget. Once again, they were a magical couple, living proof that love was indeed all you needed.

But, of course, I was wrong. The pain wasn't over at all, and things were about to get so much worse before they would finally get better. Because John's betrayal in that coat-filled room on election night turned out to be merely a prelude. It had simply lit the fuse for a far more powerful explosion to come.

John's "Lost Weekend" was about to begin.

PART THREE

CUT
PIECE

NINE

Los Angeles, 1973 to 1974

T here are those who believe Yoko not only approved of the affair but arranged it. That she planted May Pang in the seat next to John on that American Airlines flight from New York to Los Angeles knowing full well what was likely to happen. That their comely twenty-three-year-old assistant would sooner or later end up sleeping with her husband.

It's theoretically possible, I suppose. Yoko has always been a complicated woman, gaming out her future like a chess master thinking five moves ahead. It could be she saw some strategic long-term advantage in setting up the affair; by handpicking John's mistress, she might have felt she could exert some dominion over his extramarital wanderings. Perhaps, thanks to her mystical advisors, she really did see what was coming, knew that

John was heading for a free fall, and was endeavoring to soften his inevitable crash.

If any of that is true, though, Yoko never breathed a word of it to me. All she said in October of 1973 was that she was sending John and an assistant to L.A. Could I please meet them at the airport?

I was by then aware that their marriage was in deep trouble. Despite their best efforts to mend the relationship—despite all that intense nesting in their new home at the Dakota—the red light on my bedroom ceiling had been blinking even more feverishly than usual in the days and weeks leading up to what would later be known as John's "Lost Weekend," the eighteen months he spent in exile from his wife and his home in New York.

Yoko's demeanor back then, as always, was not demonstrably emotional: that's not who she's ever been, even under the stress of her collapsing marriage. But it was clear from our phone conversations that she was in pain. "John and I are not getting along very well. You know that, don't you, Elliot?" she asked during one of them.

"I'm so sorry to hear it," I said.

"We don't see each other very much. And we don't talk very much, either."

"Is there anything I can do to help?" I asked.

"What could you possibly do to help?" she answered. "John has become a distraction to my work. He doesn't understand all that I do. He just gets in the way. It gets very tiring. Sometimes I just need to be alone."

John's calls were every bit as depressing.

"Has Mother been talking to you about us?" he asked during one early morning chat.

"Yoko talks to me about everything," I answered vaguely.

"I never get to be with her anymore," he lamented. "The other day I shaved and got dressed up and told her I wanted to take her to her favorite restaurant. And she turned me down. She said she didn't have time. Me own fucking wife said that to me!"

I don't know if there was one specific moment—a particularly hurtful slight, perhaps, or an especially cross word—that finally snapped Yoko's patience. I suspect not. She has always been a methodical person, and my guess is that she precisely and carefully orchestrated John's eviction from the Dakota. She likely consulted with her team of spiritual advisors to determine the most astrologically and numerologically opportune time to begin their marital separation, then went about arranging the logistical details—his flight itinerary, his lodgings in L.A., perhaps even his female companionship—with the cool precision of a doctor preparing for an amputation. It was all so smoothly planned and executed, John might not have even realized what was happening to him.

He certainly didn't seem like a man who'd been kicked out of his home when I met him and May Pang at LAX airport.

"You look trim, Ellie!" he said with a big grin when I greeted them at the arrival gate. "Have you been taking those diet pills again?"

"Injections," I corrected him. "And, no, I haven't."

They had very little luggage, suggesting that neither of them was expecting a long stay in Los Angeles. I grabbed some of their bags and led the way to where I had parked my car. My instructions from Yoko were to drive them to music manager Lou Adler's house in Bel Air, an 8,000-square-foot mini-mansion up on Stone Canyon Road that had been borrowed for John while he was in town. A few heads turned as we quickly traversed the terminal, but in those days airports were relatively safe spaces for celebrities. (This was before paparazzi started runway stake-outs to ambush bleary-eyed stars deplaning from long, exhausting flights.)

"I need some money," John said as we settled into my weary old Jaguar. May, who had barely said a word since they'd landed, sat in the back seat. "Mother said these could be used for money," John continued, shoving a fistful of traveler's checks in my hand. It was about $10,000 worth, a sizable sum even now but a small fortune back in 1973. "Can you get money for these?"

John was functionally a child when it came to taking care of himself. This wasn't his fault: he'd been a rock star since he was a teenager. His every want had been arranged for him virtually his entire adult life. He never learned to do his own grocery shopping, never paid a utility bill or mailed a package or involved himself in any of the myriad mundane tasks the rest of us spend so much of our daily lives mired in. He was clueless about the most basic elements of human commerce, like money and how to buy stuff with it.

But then, that was what May was for. Whatever other intentions Yoko may or may not have had for the assistant, her primary job in L.A. was to make sure John was properly fed and cared for, that all his basic needs—or at least most of them—were satisfied.

A few words here about May, because over the decades she has never been shy about presenting her own version of what transpired during the Lost Weekend (or about sharing her own unflattering views about Yoko, whom she apparently perceived as her romantic rival). She's published several books about her affair with John, discussed the intimate details of it in documentaries, and given hundreds of interviews on the subject. And if you believe her account, you inevitably come away with the impression that for a time she was the red-hot center of John's universe—that their romance was the axis around which the entire Lost Weekend revolved.

I don't doubt that she believes this to be true. I suspect she was indeed deeply in love with John. And I have no reason to doubt that John harbored genuine affection for her, too. I can tell you my impression of her when I picked them up at the airport was that she was an intelligent, attractive, and highly competent young woman. She didn't smoke. She didn't drink. She struck me as potentially a superb assistant.

But I can also tell you that after I dropped her and John off at Adler's house—stopping briefly at a bank on the way to cash those traveler's checks—I seldom bumped into her again in Los

Angeles. Perhaps even more tellingly, in all the years I knew John—all the way up to his final days—I cannot recall a single conversation in which he ever mentioned her name.

So I will let May tell her own story in her own way in her own books. In this one, I will leave her for now at the front door of Adler's house in Bel Air, escorting her employer's husband inside, while I pull away in my Jag, heading back to Laurel Canyon, watching the two of them disappear in my rearview mirror. To this day, I only wish her well.

Twenty or so minutes later, when I opened the door to my own home, I could hear the phone ringing. It was, of course, the hotline. Yoko was calling.

"Did everything go okay?" she asked.

"Yes, they arrived safely. I got the traveler's checks cashed for him and took them to Lou Adler's house. Everything went smoothly."

"How did he appear?" Yoko asked.

"You mean physically?"

"You know what I mean, Elliot. Did he appear happy?"

"He just appeared like John."

"Are you withholding anything from me?"

"Yoko, I want to make something clear. I love you. And I love John. And I will not take sides. I'm not going to withhold anything from either of you. If there's something you don't want John to know, just don't tell me. Because I'm not comfortable keeping secrets from either of you."

There was a long pause before she spoke again.

"Just keep him safe, Elliot. Can you do that for me? Can you keep him safe?"

"I'll do everything I can," I answered.

FOR the first few months, John appeared entirely content in Los Angeles—one might even say gleeful. He seemed to consider his expulsion from the Dakota and banishment to the West Coast as something of a bachelor's holiday. Remember, he was twenty-one when he married Cynthia; he was twenty-eight when he married Yoko. Now, at the cusp of thirty-three, for the first time in his adult life, he didn't have a wife (or, for that matter, three other partners) who made up his extended family. He was a free man.

His spirits were certainly high when, a couple of weeks into his L.A. stay, I filmed him during a stroll along the Malibu shoreline. He had a new album coming out, *Mind Games*, and was anxious to publicize it, so he'd agreed to do another interview with me. But rather than putting him on my radio show again, I asked John if he'd be interested in letting me talk to him on camera for a segment on KABC TV's *Eyewitness News*.

"We could do it on the beach," I suggested, knowing how much John enjoyed the call of the ocean. "It'd be nice to take in some sea air."

John quickly agreed, but I started having second thoughts the minute I began planning out the details. Would I need a permit to shoot on the beach? What about crowd control: How to make sure we weren't mobbed by onlookers? Which beach should we tape at? Which was the least crowded? And what sort of equipment would we need? In those days, a portable news camera was a gigantic contraption that sat on a cameraman's shoulder. The battery pack was even bigger and was worn like a knapsack on the operator's back. Separate sound equipment would be required as well: capturing TV-quality audio on a windy beach filled with the ambient sounds of crashing waves was a lot harder than it looked.

In the end, though, I decided to just wing it. I picked up John at Lou's house around noon and headed to Malibu in the Jag, a small crew following close behind in a TV news van. I figured we'd drive along the coast until we found a beachy spot that looked hospitable and simply shoot the interview guerrilla-style, with no permits or crowd control, just the element of surprise working in our favor. Hopefully, the cameraman and sound operator would know what needed to be done.

"Have you eaten anything?" I asked John as I drove, making conversation.

"I had a cup of tea, nothing else," he said. "I could go for a bite."

As it happened, there was a McDonald's just down the road—I could see its giant golden arches—so I signaled the van behind us that we were going to make a brief pit stop. For some reason, this McDonald's parking lot was nearly deserted, which I counted as a lucky break. The last thing I needed was for John to get mobbed by fans even before the interview started.

"Tell me what you want, and I'll pick it up; you stay in the car," I told John after I swung into one of the empty spaces.

"What do they have?" he asked. "Bangers and mash? That would do me well."

And here, I confess, I was at something of a loss. I had never eaten at a McDonald's before (or, for that matter, since). I had heard the term "Big Mac" but was not entirely sure what it meant. I was confident, however, that bangers and mash were not on the menu.

"It's hamburgers and French fries—that sort of thing," I said.

"Whatever you call them, Ellie, that'll be fine," he said, glancing around at the empty parking lot with a curious glint in his eyes.

Then, before I could open my car door, John put his hand on my arm.

"I haven't driven a car in a while," he said. "Do you think I could drive yours around here for a bit?"

It was no secret that John was a notoriously terrible driver. Although he'd passed a British driving test in 1965, at the height of Beatlemania, he'd spent almost no time behind the wheel. On those few occasions when he did drive, he was famously poor at navigating roads and even worse at noticing other traffic. In fact, just four years earlier, in 1969, while holidaying in Scotland, he'd been in a horrendous accident, crashing and rolling his Austin Maxi into a roadside ditch.

I gulped down hard. I thought about my promise to Yoko to keep him safe. But I knew John well enough not to argue with him. Besides, the lot was so empty, what could go wrong? I nodded and motioned for him to switch places with me.

"Are you sure you can handle this?" I asked nervously from the passenger seat as he fiddled with the shifter.

"Just you watch," he answered overconfidently.

And with that, John jammed his foot on the accelerator and sent the car shooting through the lot like an off-course rocket. I could feel the g-forces plunging me into the back of my seat as we caromed around the asphalt. John jerked the wheel wildly to the right, sending me slamming against the passenger door. Then, just as wildly, he yanked the wheel to the left, nearly flinging the Jag into a 360-degree spinout. Finally, after what felt like an eternity, he pounded on the brakes and came to a screeching halt, filling the air with the smell of burning tire rubber. In my side mirror, I could see the camera guys standing by the TV van across the lot, staring at us with their mouths wide-open.

"Well," I said after catching my breath, "how did that feel?"

"I think your steering wheel needs adjustment," John said.

My steering wheel was fine. My neck, on the other hand . . .

The interview, in the end, turned out great. After carefully pulling out of the McDonald's lot, I cautiously navigated to a surprisingly desolate stretch of beach near the Malibu pier, where the camera crew taped John and me talking about everything from his new album to his memories of Beatlemania to the ultimate question on everybody's mind—and the one John had been asked at least a thousand times before: the possibility of a Beatles reunion.

"It's quite possible, yes," he said as we sat on the sand. "I don't know why the hell we'd do it, but it's possible."

"Would you like that to happen?" I pressed.

"If it happens, I'll enjoy it."

"Would you want to initiate that to happen?"

"Well, I couldn't say."

"But if you could, is it something you'd like to see yourself doing?"

"I don't know, Ellie. You know me: I go on instinct. If the idea hit me tomorrow, I might call them and say, 'Come on, let's do something.' So, I couldn't really tell you. If it happens, it'll happen."

"So it's not something you would totally rule out as never taking place?"

"No, no, my memories are now all fond and the wounds have all healed. If we do it, we do it. If we record, we record."

When it aired later that night, it seemed as if the entire city of Los Angeles—and beyond—had watched. It was by far the most well-received interview I'd ever done or ever would do. In fact, about the only person I knew who didn't watch it was John.

"Why would I watch it?" he said when I asked what he thought of the broadcast. "I was there when you filmed it."

JOHN and I spent a lot of time together over the next several weeks and months. And when we didn't see each other in person, we kept up our regular phone calls. But he was also expanding his friendship circle in L.A., hanging out with people like Harry Nilsson, the brilliant but notoriously hell-raising singer-songwriter, who was quickly becoming one of John's best drinking buddies. In fact, a few weeks after our TV interview on the beach, John called to tell me he wanted to fly up to Vegas to party with some of his new pals. Could I take him there?

It was clear he wasn't inviting me to join them; rather, he needed an escort to make the journey with him and get him to whatever hotel—it might have been the Flamingo, or perhaps Caesars Palace; I don't remember—had been designated as their meeting spot. But I said yes anyway because . . . well, because John asked me.

So, the next day, at 10:00 a.m.—an ungodly hour on my timetable—I picked up John at Adler's house and drove him to LAX, where even in those days there were hourly flights to Vegas. About halfway to the airport, though, on a particularly sketchy stretch of La Cienega Boulevard, John spotted something that made his eyes go big: It was a sorry little strip joint called the Losers.

"We need to stop there, Ellie," he said. "We need to check out the Losers."

I glanced over at him and saw that he was serious. Against my better judgment, I pulled the car into the club's lot, where there were three or four other parked cars. I tried to imagine what sort of people might be compelled to frequent such a seedy establishment at 10:30 in the morning . . . until I realized we were about to become two of them. Then, as I so often did when wandering in public with John, I began mentally calculating the likelihood of a crowd situation. I remembered the mob John drew the last time he'd put us in a similar situation, when he'd asked me to take him to see *Deep Throat* at the Pussycat Theatre on Hollywood Boulevard. We had to elbow through hundreds of grabby autograph seekers before finally getting through the doors and taking our seats for the 5:45 showing. (John, by the way, didn't care for the film; we left after twenty minutes. "I had much better," he noted dryly on the drive home.)

But here's the thing about fame that I learned that morning during our brief stopover at the Losers: context is everything. The odds of an artist of John Lennon's stature turning up in a place this sad and dreary were so astronomically remote that when he *did* show up, nobody could believe it. Even the weary dancer performing on the stage inches away from him—staring straight into his easily recognizable face—couldn't bring herself to make the connection. She might have thought, *Hey, this guy looks a lot like John Lennon*, but I doubt she suspected for a second that she really was dancing for the genius who wrote "Strawberry Fields Forever."

We spent maybe thirty depressing minutes at the Losers, dropping quarters in the jukebox in the corner, watching as the morning shift dancers listlessly gyrated and struggled to remove their bikini tops, before resuming our trip to the airport. As we left, John smiled and softly sang an all-too-appropriate lyric from one of the songs on *Some Time in New York City*: "*We make her paint her face and dance . . .*"

After we landed in Vegas and arrived at the hotel, I witnessed the flip side of the context of fame. Unlike a seedy topless club on La Cienega, a fancy hotel casino on the Strip was an entirely plausible place for a celebrity like John Lennon to be spotted—which is why it was completely predictable that John would set off a stampede when he stopped for a few spins at the roulette wheel.

He was demonstrating a "can't lose" gambling system he had developed on his own. Using $300 that he borrowed from me—once again, I was reminded of and amused to see how bad John was with money and how odd it was that he never carried his own cash—he was placing one-chip bets on all but one of the numbers on the table. Of course, with that big a spread, one of John's numbers nearly always came up, which he took as proof that his system was infallible. When I tried to explain that he was losing money on every spin—the casino paid him thirty-five chips for every winning bet, but it was costing him thirty-seven chips to nearly cover the table—he just stared back at me, indignant.

"But I'm winning every time!" he exclaimed.

I never got the chance to unpack the flaw in his gaming logic because, within a matter of minutes, the roulette table was overrun by fans waving napkins and pens in John's face, demanding autographs. "The Beatles are here! The Beatles are here!" someone in the casino shouted, triggering an even larger surge around us. I grabbed John by the arm and steered him through the throng until we found a phalanx of hotel security guards, who pulled

John behind them and escorted him to safety. I followed closely behind, making sure John was okay. After a brief, reassuring conversation with the hotel staff, I felt confident he would get to his appointment with his friends.

I had done what had been requested of me. I had delivered John to Vegas. There wasn't much else for me to do, so I turned around, took a cab back to the airport, hopped on a plane, and was back in Laurel Canyon a few hours later.

Again, within minutes of opening my door, the hotline started ringing.

"How is he?" Yoko asked.

"He's fine," I told her. "He's in Las Vegas meeting some friends."

"Which friends? Who is he meeting?"

"I'm not entirely sure," I answered truthfully. "He didn't really say. I'm guessing maybe Harry Nilsson. They've been hanging out a lot."

Yoko was silent for a beat.

"Keep trying to keep him safe, Elliot."

Once again, I promised I would try.

As time went on, however, keeping John safe became a far more complicated task. After three or four months in L.A., much of his initial enthusiasm had boiled off and his mood was starting to curdle. He was missing Yoko: he began asking me when I thought she'd be ready for him to come home, a question I could never answer. He started spending more and more time with

Nilsson, drinking at the Troubadour till all hours, often shutting the place down. After John famously got thrown out for drunkenly heckling the Smothers Brothers—I wasn't there during that incident, but the next day, at John's request, I sent a large floral arrangement to the brothers as an apology—the late-night shenanigans moved from the Troubadour to the Rainbow Bar & Grill on Sunset. That's where John and Harry and a collection of others—including my old pals Micky Dolenz and Alice Cooper, as well as former Beatles road manager Mal Evans, songwriter Bernie Taupin, and musicians Keith Allison, Klaus Voormann, and Marc Bolan—formed an infamous drinking club known as the Hollywood Vampires.

It would be difficult to exaggerate the level of unbridled indulgences that took place in the Rainbow's VIP room, a small alcove atop some stairs overlooking the bar. The amount of alcohol imbibed was staggering, to say the least, and there were also small bags of cocaine discreetly passed into the room. Nilsson, a great big bear of a man, could pound down a dozen or so Brandy Alexanders—a potent mix of brandy and cream, his cocktail of choice, which John soon adopted as his own—in a single sitting. Not being a celebrity, I was never invited to become a member of the Hollywood Vampires, but I was a welcome visitor and spent many a late night on the edges of their wild, sometimes harrowing saturnalias.

"What are you drinking?" Nilsson asked me when John first introduced us.

"Um, a glass of Chardonnay would be nice," I told him.

He signaled a waiter and ordered a full bottle.

"Oh, I'll only drink a glass or two," I protested. "I've already had a couple."

John leaned into my ear and whispered, "Tonight, you're drinkin' the whole fuckin' bottle." I was reminded once again of why Yoko worried so much about John and alcohol: this wasn't a side of him either of us ever wanted to see.

There was always a crowd of attractive young women at the bottom of the steps leading to the Vampires' VIP lair, waiting for a chance to snag an interlude with a rock star. Frankly, though, by the time the boys descended, usually at closing time, most of them were too wasted to take advantage of the opportunity. I lost count of the number of times I all but carried John down those stairs and poured him into whatever car service I had called to the bar's parking lot.

For the most part, I kept my promise to Yoko: I kept John safe. But one night about three or four months into the Lost Weekend, I realized things were starting to spiral out of my control. Normally, John didn't put up much of a fight when I helped him down the stairs at the Rainbow Bar; even when completely drunk, he knew when the party was over. But on this occasion, he resisted. He didn't want to go home. He demanded to keep going even though the bar was closing, its patrons spilling out the doors. He pushed away and dove straight into the crowd in the parking lot, a throng filled with folks every bit as inebriated as he was. It was an incredibly dangerous situation, my worst nightmare, a drunken star lost inside a drunken mob.

I dove into the swarm after him, jostling through knots of revelers, desperately searching for any sign of him, growing more and more frantic. Finally, I spotted John with Nilsson at the edge of the lot, the two of them climbing into the back of a black limousine. A moment later, the limo pulled away into the night, going I had no idea where.

John, I realized with a sinking feeling in my gut, was slipping away.

TEN

Los Angeles, 1974

D o you know who Phil Spector is?"

This was John asking. A few days after disappearing into the night with Harry Nilsson, he'd resurfaced with a noon-time call. Whatever mischief he'd gotten himself into after closing the Rainbow didn't seem to have done much damage. He sounded in good spirits and relatively sober.

"Oh, I know Phil Spector," I replied. "I knew him before *you* knew him."

Spector, of course, was the legendary music producer (and future convicted murderer; more on that later) who worked with the Beatles on their last album together, 1970's *Let It Be*, and then went on to coproduce John's *Imagine*. But I first met Spector back in 1966, when I was still a fledgling radio broadcaster. The actor Sal Mineo, who'd been a pal since I interviewed him for my college station a few years earlier (and who remained a good friend until his own murder in 1976; more on that later, too), introduced us at a memorial service for Lenny Bruce, of all places.

If this book were a movie, right about now the screen would get all wavy as we dissolve into a flashback. You'd see Sal and me sitting together in a back row of Bruce's internment services at Eden Memorial Park, a Jewish cemetery in Mission Hills, California, where the seminal stand-up comedian was being laid to rest after dying of a morphine overdose at age forty. I'm not quite certain how Sal knew Lenny Bruce, although my guess is that his *Rebel Without a Cause* costar James Dean might have had something to do with it, as Dean and Bruce were known to have been friends. In any case, there were all of fifteen people attending Bruce's service, including Sal and me, a pathetic turnout for such a towering cultural figure.

But delivering the eulogy was a diminutive twenty-six-year-old man with shoulder-length dark hair and an intense, wild gaze. This was Spector, who just months earlier had produced what would turn out to be Bruce's final comedy album. Spector had obviously been profoundly impacted by Bruce's death: he didn't merely speak at the funeral; it turned out he paid for it.

Afterwards, Sal introduced us.

"I'm a big fan of your music," I told him. It was true. Many of the hits Spector had written or cowritten when he was just a teenager—"To Know Him, Is to Love Him," "Chapel of Love,"

"Da Doo Ron Ron"—had been part of the soundtrack of my own adolescence.

Spector shook my hand and stared into my eyes, sizing me up.

"Glad you're here," he finally said. "I'm certain more people will be coming."

Sadly, he was wrong about that.

After Bruce's funeral, Phil and I became unlikely friends. We'd hang out often at Dino's Lodge, a nightspot on Sunset Boulevard owned by Dean Martin, which at the time was famous as a location on the TV series *77 Sunset Strip*. (It was where the character Kookie, played by Edd Byrnes, worked as a parking valet.) Or else I'd drive over to Phil's house in Beverly Hills—one of his starter mansions—and while away the hours listening to his spellbinding but often bizarre conspiracy theories, including the one in which he maintained that the government was responsible for Bruce's death.

Spector was, to put it mildly, an eccentric figure, prone to paranoia and other delusions. His house was filled with guns. There wasn't a tabletop, countertop, or other surface that didn't have a firearm on it. Even when he wasn't home—when, say, we were dining at Dino's Lodge—he was always armed with a pistol; you could see his hand fidgeting with a shoulder holster under his jacket whenever he was in mental distress, which was often. Somehow, though, I had a knack for calming him. I'd just ask him to look into my eyes while I soothingly assured him that everything was going to be all right.

It's odd, I know, that over the years I've found myself in the company of so many famous people. None would consume me nearly as completely as John and Yoko, but there were plenty of others hovering around the edges of my life. Beyond Sal and Phil and my pals in Laurel Canyon—as well as the scores I'd interview on my radio show—there would be lots more celebrity attachments in my future, from Paris Hilton to Baba Ram Dass.

Exactly why this happens to me, I cannot tell you. I never sought out relationships with famous people; they just somehow gravitated towards me. I obviously wasn't famous myself, but as a radio host I swam in famous waters, which put me in their lane. However, whatever they saw in me that made them want to be my friend—a safe connection to the civilian world, perhaps, or some sort of intuited misfit kinship—has always remained a mystery to me. In my more mystical moments, I sometimes ponder if all of us were bound by an Akashic agreement, a "soul contract" that made our friendships cosmically inevitable, forever to be repeated in various incarnations for all eternity.

Of course, it could just be the luck of the draw, the same spinning wheel of chance that determines so many of the twists and turns of our lives. But the connections among my acquaintances sometimes seemed so fated—occasionally fateful—that it begged an explanation beyond happenstance. For instance, the fact that I was friends with Phil was odd in itself; the fact that I would also become intimate friends—borderline soul mates—with Lana Clarkson, the actress whom Phil would shoot in 2003 and, in 2009, be convicted of killing in his Pyrenees Castle in

Alhambra . . . well, that just seems to me far too tragically syn-chronous to be a random act of chance.

But now the screen is getting wavy again as we return to late 1973, to John on the phone asking if I knew who Phil Spector was. He explained that he was recording an album of classic '50s pop tunes with Spector at his studio in Hollywood. "I've always wanted to do an oldies-but-moldies kind of album," he said. "I liked those songs when I was a kid, before I had even written one of me own. There was a sort of innocence about them, like 'Ain't That a Shame.' Did you know that was the first song I ever learned?"

"I didn't know that, John."

"Yeah, me mum taught it to me on a banjo before I learned the guitar. Do you want to come to the studio later and hang out? We're at a place called A&M on La Brea Avenue. Do you know it?"

"Yes," I responded, "it's the old Charlie Chaplin studio. I'll be there."

The Spector Sessions, as they came to be known, were among the most notorious jams in rock 'n' roll history. I ended up spend-ing about half a dozen all-nighters at these riotous, drug- and alcohol-fueled bacchanals, occasionally finding myself in the un-enviable position of having to tidy up some of the messes after-wards. I wasn't there (thank goodness) the night Spector famously fired a gun into the ceiling, but I saw plenty of other harrowing incidents. It's amazing to me that nobody ended up seriously injured. Even more astonishing was that such a profoundly won-derful album—*Rock 'n' Roll*—came out on the other end of all that chaos and debauchery.

As I recall, though, the Spector Sessions didn't start out quite so raucous. In fact, when I popped in for my first visit, driving over from the radio station after my show ended at 11:00 p.m., the mood at the studio was decidedly sleepy, if a bit boozy. There was practically no security on duty at that hour— just a tired nightwatchman slouched in a chair at the front gate, reading a magazine. John was inside the recording room, impatiently waiting for Spector, who stood at the control console adjusting levers, to give the signal for him to start singing. I was only mildly surprised to see Phil dressed in a butcher's white outfit. He often wore what he referred to as "disguises." Wigs were not uncommon. He liked to dress up.

Spector nodded at me when I caught his eye and waved me over. It was obvious he was a little drunk.

"Good to see you," he slurred. "We're about to lay down some important tracks."

"How's John doing?" I asked.

"It's slow with him, but he'll fall into the groove."

John saw me from inside the recording area and signaled me to come over. It was obvious he, too, was a little buzzed.

"How's it going?" I asked.

"Very slow, mate," he said. "This bugger moves at his own speed. The butcher has kept us waiting hours."

John offered me a swig from a bottle of whiskey he seemed to conjure out of thin air. I waved it away and found a comfortable spot to sit while I waited for the recording to commence. And waited. And waited some more.

John didn't get a chance to sing a single note that night. After a couple of hours fiddling at the control console, Spector announced it was a wrap and slipped out the door without another word. John and the other musicians looked at each other, shrugged their shoulders, and started filing out of the studio into the parking lot. Everyone was drunk, or high, or both.

When I returned a few nights later, however, it was a very different scene. As if a switch had been flipped, Spector's sleepy studio was now buzzing with activity. Indeed, it was suddenly the biggest party in Hollywood, a full-on "happening." Warren Beatty, Elton John, Cher, Joni Mitchell, David Geffen—everywhere I looked I spotted another superstar who'd come to watch John Lennon perform. And this time he most certainly did get a chance to sing. Stepping up to the microphone, John belted out such a heart-wrenching cover of "To Know Him Is to Love Him," he left the whole room speechless. John's voice sounded so rich, so intimately familiar with the lyrics, you could tell the song ran through his veins.

Phil, meanwhile, stood at the controls, wearing what appeared to be a woman's blond wig, beaming drunkenly at the crowd.

But the rock gods giveth and taketh. A couple of nights later, the switch flipped again, and the energy at Phil's studio turned from celebratory to poisonous. I arrived to find John and Phil arguing and cursing at each other as sullen crew musicians glowered at them from the sidelines. Both John and Phil were clearly loaded; Phil could barely stand. Some of the studio artists grew so fed up with the rancor, they stormed out of the session. Nothing got recorded that night.

THE sessions frequently broke up just before dawn, although their malignant vibe seemed to follow John around like a toxic cloud even when he wasn't at the studio. Sometimes, after they finished, I'd drive a barely conscious John home to Lou Adler's house, all but carrying him to the door. On one memorable occasion, though, he was just awake enough to stop off for a bite at a place I knew on Sunset. It was a cozy, wood-paneled bistro, the Aware Inn, that never attracted much of an early morning crowd, so it felt relatively safe. Besides, after an all-nighter with Phil, John was barely recognizable.

He entered the restaurant wearing dark sunglasses, looking unshaven, unkempt, and unwashed. He desperately needed fresh air—he was running on alcohol fumes and cocaine embers—so I grabbed a table outside on the patio. I sat facing the direction of Hollywood, keeping a lookout for paparazzi and overeager fans; John sat facing Beverly Hills, slouched in his metal chair, his hands shaking a bit as he chain-smoked. We were both groggy and quiet.

Then she appeared.

She was a stunning Black woman, tall and curvaceous. Under her arm she was carrying a portfolio, suggesting she was either a model or an actress getting an early start on a day full of auditions. "Excuse me," she said softly, flipping a strand of long dark hair from her mesmerizing emerald-green eyes, "I don't mean to inter-

rupt. But this is my phone number. Use it whenever you're ready."
She slipped a small piece of paper next to John's plate. Then she
turned as if on a catwalk and sashayed away from us. John peered
over his sunglasses, watching her leave. He picked up the paper,
gave it a quick glance, and tossed it over to me. I put it in my
pocket, as I generally did when this sort of thing happened, which
it did from time to time, usually never to be mentioned again.

Which is why, a few days later, I was a little surprised when
John brought up the breakfast girl during one of our calls.

"Remember that good-looking bird who left her number for
me?" he asked. "You still got it? I've got a night off from recording
and thought I'd give her a call."

"I keep everything that's handed to you, John. That's why I
have such big pockets."

In fact, I did keep every scrap of paper that was handed to
him—notes from strangers pitching song ideas, fan letters from
Beatle devotees, phone numbers from groupies—mainly because
I thought it was rude to leave them behind. Usually I'd toss them
out a day or two later. I could never recall a single time when
John asked about any of them . . . until now.

It felt a little awkward—after all, John knew I was Yoko's best
friend—but I scrambled around, looking for the jacket I'd been
wearing, fished out the piece of paper, and read John the name and
number. After all, he was a grown man, separated from his wife,
free to do as he pleased. He could phone whomever he wanted.

Except, the very next morning, I was startled awake by the
flashing hotline: John was calling in a panic.

"What are you doing?" he asked, his voice sounding like gravel.

"I'm sleeping," I said. "What do you need?"

"I need you to get over here right away. I've got a problem."

"Are you in danger?" I asked.

"We're all in danger," he said. "Just get over here." He gave me an address—different from Lou Adler's house—then the line went dead.

I threw on some clothes and prayed the Jag would start without too much trouble, which, for once, it did. A few minutes later I was in Beverly Hills, pulling into the driveway of a small boutique hotel. How John had ended up here for a date with the breakfast girl, I will never know; he didn't know how to check himself in and I'm certain May Pang didn't make the arrangements. But when I walked into the suite I found the actress-model sitting on the sofa, looking exquisite in a terry cloth robe. We nodded hello to each other, and I hurried down the hallway to the bedroom, where John was sitting on the mattress, half-dressed, with his head in his hands.

"Get rid of her," he ordered, barely looking up at me.

"Excuse me?" I said.

"Elliot, I want her out of here. Get her out."

I wasn't happy about it—being John's morning-after cleanup crew was never a role I envisioned for myself—but after a few more words I headed back to the living room to see if I could diplomatically dislodge John's overnight guest, who by now was out of the robe and climbing back into her clothing.

"Hi," I said. "I'm a friend of our friend. We met at breakfast the other day. Do you need a ride somewhere? Can I call you a cab?"

"Don't worry, honey," she said as she hoisted an overnight bag onto her slender shoulder. "I'm on my way out. No problems from me."

We did not say goodbye as she walked out the door.

I returned to the bedroom, where John was smoking a cigarette.

"Is she gone?" he asked.

"Yeah," I answered, a bit miffed. "But, John, I need you to know that I did not feel comfortable doing that. Please don't ask me ever to do anything like that again. That's not the sort of business I'm in."

John shot me a stare, his eyes icy cold.

"I'm gonna ask you to do anything I fucking feel like asking you," he sneered through gritted teeth. "Don't you ever tell me what I can or can't say to you. You hear me?"

Yoko had warned me that John could be an altogether different person when he was drinking—I'd already seen evidence of that—but this was different. He'd never talked to me like that before, never turned the heat ray of his anger on me with such intensity.

I walked out of the bedroom, closed the living room curtains, and left. The minute I got home, I could see the blinking red hotline flashing in the bedroom. I didn't know if it was John or Yoko, and at that moment I didn't really care. For the first time, I decided to let it keep blinking.

For the next week or so, I avoided the recording sessions and didn't talk to John at all, even on the phone. Although Yoko and I continued to speak regularly, I never told her anything about John's dalliance with the breakfast girl or how terribly he had treated me. I wasn't comfortable keeping secrets from her, but I also wasn't eager to snitch on her husband.

Instead, Yoko and I talked about other matters, like her gallery openings and her own musical performances during John's long absence from her life. I remember one rather poignant late-night phone call about, of all things, mah-jongg.

"Do you know the game, Elliot?" she asked me.

"Yes, my mother used to play it. It's like chess but with little ivory tiles."

"No, it's not like chess at all," she said. "But the other day I was playing with some of my friends . . ."

I tried to picture who those friends might be, remembering the group of elderly Jewish women who played mah-jongg with my mother in our little living room in Washington Heights. Somehow, I was having a hard time visualizing Yoko in that sort of scene.

". . . and I was winning all the games," she went on. "We were betting small amounts of money, and I kept winning every time."

"Well, that doesn't sound too bad," I said, surprised to learn that Yoko was betting money. She had often criticized me for my own propensity for gambling.

"Except none of them paid me," she continued. "They all left without giving me any money."

"Was it a lot of money?"

"No, but it's the principle of it, Elliot. It's just like with presents. You know how I love to give people presents, don't you?"

"Yes," I said, thinking of all the lovely presents she and John had given me since we'd met, including cherished art pieces that she and John had crafted together as birthday gifts.

"I don't receive presents. People don't give me anything. They just assume there's nothing I would like to have that I can't buy for myself, so they don't even engage in the gesture."

"John gives you lots of presents," I noted, trying to make her feel better.

"Well, John isn't here right now, is he?" she said.

No, he most definitely was not. In fact, where John was at that very moment—and what he was doing—was a matter that was about to become painfully clear to me. Because not long after Yoko hung up the phone, it rang again, sending me racing in the middle of the night to Lou Adler's house, where I would encounter a version of John I hardly recognized. I was about to walk into the nadir of the Lost Weekend, John's rock bottom.

The call came not on the hotline but my regular house phone, and the voice on the other end identified himself as a security officer working for Phil Spector. John was in trouble: Could I please hurry over to Adler's house and help "calm him down."

What I saw when I stepped into Adler's living room some twenty minutes later looked like a scene out of *The Exorcist*. Drunk and wild-eyed, John was strapped to a high-backed chair, his arms and legs restrained with ropes, which he was struggling against with all his might as he seethed and shouted obscenities at his captors, a pair of beefy-armed bodyguards who stood in awkward silence nearby. The place was a shambles. John had torn some of Adler's framed gold records off the walls—and there were many of them: Adler managed or had managed Carole King, the Mamas and the Papas, Neil Young, Cass Elliot, Cheech and Chong, and Sam Cooke, among a slew of others—and had smashed them to pieces. Bits of broken wood and shattered plexiglass littered the floor.

Where May Pang might have been, I have no idea. I didn't see any sign of her.

From what I heard from the security guards, the meltdown had started earlier that evening at the studio, where John and Phil had nearly come to blows. What precisely they were arguing about, nobody seemed to remember. But the session ended early with Phil's guards restraining John and shuttling him to Adler's house, where John slipped away from them long enough to pick up some sort of walking stick or cane, which he swung wildly around the living room until the guards were able to subdue him again and strap him to the chair.

I paused before slowly stepping up to John, two or three feet away, looking him up and down, searching for any cuts or bruises or damage that might require medical attention. He had stopped shouting for the moment. His head hung low on his shoulders, his face pointed to the floor, his chest heaving furiously, as if he were having trouble catching his breath. After a long beat, he slowly lifted his eyes to me. He looked possessed.

"You!" he snarled. "What are you doing here?"

"John, are you okay?" I asked softly, testing the waters.

"Get these ropes off me!" he erupted. "Get them off me, you . . ."

And then John spat out an epithet so hurtful and offensive—so obviously fueled by drunken rage—I can't bring myself to repeat it.

Suffice to say nobody in my entire life had ever talked to me that way, much less somebody I considered a dear friend. I couldn't believe this was the same man who'd written and sung so powerfully about peace and love and understanding. I looked straight into his eyes, barely containing my disgust and disappointment. He looked back into mine. And that exchange of glances seemed to reach some shred of humanity buried deep in John's alcohol-addled brain. Suddenly he became very, very quiet. Whatever fever had been simmering inside his troubled soul seemed finally to break.

After a moment or two, I turned to the guards. "I think you can take those ropes off of him," I said. "I think he's done."

They looked at each other, not certain what to do. "Are you sure, Mr. Mintz?"

I nodded, and they began to untie him. John stood up, rubbed his wrists, and, without another word, slowly made his way down the hall to the bedroom, where he must have collapsed on the mattress and passed out.

The next day, as I was getting ready to leave for work, the hotline started flashing. I thought about letting it go—I was exhausted, had barely slept, with John's slur-filled tirade running through my mind all night—but in the end, for whatever reason, I decided to pick up the phone.

"Ellie?" John said.

"Yes, John."

"I'm sorry for what I said."

"Uh-huh," I replied.

"But if you think about it, if that's the worst thing I could say about you, you couldn't be all that bad, right?"

"Thanks for the compliment," I said.

"Well, welcome to the real world, Mother Virgin Mary. I'm me. I have a big mouth and express meself the way I feel when I feel it. I don't hide behind some microphone. I sing into it or speak into it when it suits me. I'm not always the 'Imagine' guy, or the 'Jealous Guy,' or the 'Walrus.' So I said I'm sorry to you. That's all I can do."

He waited a beat for my response.

"Do you want to have dinner?" he went on when there was none.

"No," I answered. "I think I'm going to take the night off."

And then, for the first time I can remember, I was the one who hung up the phone without saying so much as goodbye.

1973:
This collage was made for me by John and Yoko for my birthday, and is meant to represent different parts of me and of our relationship. It was the first gift they ever gave to me.

Courtesy of the author

```
                                             1 west 72 nynynyny
                                             wed jewn 73.
     dear elliot,

               as you can see.I'm learning to type.you ars receiving a letter.

     I am writing it.That makes two of us.anyway que pasa ?as they say in

     prison.I see SAL did it again!we might be down your way soon for the

     dykes balls.meaning yoko id going to prison.(to perform )xI will be s

     upporting her like a bra,(but not as a master musiker),meaning I.11

     be hanging around looking serious with me portapak video which reveals

     ALL.(beware the lennin)I wonder if one has freudian slips in a typeweiter?

     Iwonder if one has freydian lips on an afghan hound?all thede questiond

     and more will be answered a somertime in the future.(which is just around

     the corner.)
                Yoko has just woken up.someone has stopped practising in

     ca central park.thesw two things happened at the same time.upi.you will

     inf undwer stand the deeper meaning behind thedsw two appwarantly yyu

     unrelated occurances,.The massage is simple,

                          que sera aaaa"!

                          yoxxxinxexexxx

                          your interesting friend,

                          j.f .lennonononono.

                          (jog)john.
     ps. im having a ps. because i'm enjoying himself.;
     nb.i'mlooking over the 1 park.pweople aerd rowing,trees aeare greening.
     for me am muy gal.
```

June 1973:

John learns to type—not very well—in one of a hundred or more

playful letters and cards he sent me over the years.

Courtesy of the author

Circa 1975:
John and I on an afternoon sailing voyage around the New York coastline. John loved the sea—he grew up in a port city. So, he was in his element that day.

Courtesy of the author

Circa 1975:
John and I in the Dakota's living room, improvising on the white Steinway (the very same piano John played in the famous *Imagine* video).

Courtesy of the author

1975:

A card signed "Shingo," one of John's dozens of whimsical alter egos.
"Sgt. Swade" and "The Great Wok" were among the others.

Courtesy of the author

LENNON MUSIC
1370 AVENUE OF THE AMERICAS
NEW YORK, NEW YORK 10019
212-586-6444
TELEX: 148315

Dear Eliot,

What are you doing?You naughty little surfer!For heavens(?)
sake dont go back down the drain,as it were,(was).Dont kid yourself about
'handling it better'...try and stick with wine at least my dear.
We'll probably have talked to you by the time you get this.Didnt realize
how long it's bin since we talked.THE NUMBER IS _____,by the way.
Tell Sunshine I'm ex-comunicating with anyone I met in the time I was
separated from Yoko...I have meditated long and deep...and this is my
final decision (nothing personal Billy,of course!).If this doesnt suit,
maybe an old fashioned FUCK OFF will do the trick.The trouble with all
those kinda freeks is once they smell 'fear'..i.e.discomfort...they move
in on all of us.I have a feeling his bark is worse than his wife!
If your young friend is loosing interest in the book...didnt you get
paid anything yet?...There's always use for the stuff in the form of
'articles'in places like england and japan...?

I'm doing a book meself ,old chum,a sort of In
His Own Garbarge...with the second sight of 34/5 years up my scrotum!
It's good fun while I'm waiting for the genious to be born.O.K.!O.K.!
WE'RE WAITING!!

That's all fer now...

dont do it...

you were only just getting your life/health back..

why ruin it out of 'boredom'...

leave that to those other idiots out there..

or it's errol flynn/tracy/bogart/hello etc..and
WHO WANTS TO BE THAT DUMB!!!!!!!!!!!!!!!

lovey dovey the onolennons.

1975:
Another letter from John, this one referencing a planned autobiography,
which he ultimately never got around to writing.

Courtesy of the author

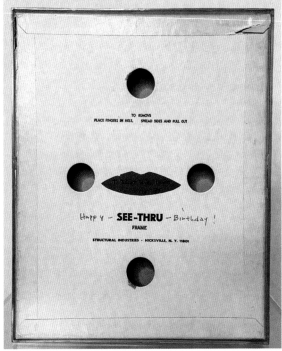

1975:

A collage that Yoko made for me on what
she called my "see-thru" birthday.

Courtesy of the author

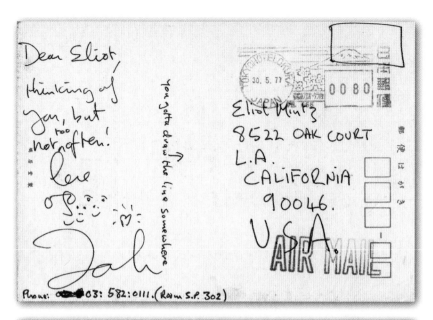

May 30, 1977:
One of John's postcards from Japan,
sent before I joined him and Yoko in Karuizawa
for several weeks of rest, relaxation, and alarmingly fresh sushi.

On the reverse side of the postcard was this charming drawing
by John. Yoko clearly wasn't the only visual artist in the family.
John sent me hundreds of doodles and drawings over the
years, including this one of him and his family (and a sheep).

Courtesy of the author

1977:
At a restaurant in Kyoto, where turtle soup was served
in the turtle's actual shell. I didn't ask for seconds.

1977:
John, Yoko, and I visit a Shinto temple in Kyoto, where we followed
the local tradition of hanging our horoscopes on a line.

1977:
Outside the Mampei, the hotel where John, Yoko,
Sean, and I stayed while sojourning in Karuizawa.

1977: Another shot taken at the Shinto temple in Kyoto.

Photographs by Nishi F. Saimaru, courtesy of Ms. Saimaru and the author.

1977:
John sent me this photo of Ringo Starr and Mae West (who starred together in Mae's final film, a musical comedy called *Sextette*), annotated with a few helpful notes.

Courtesy of the author

1978:

John would sometimes send me his version of a koan, a Japanese riddle designed to make you think. I never did solve this particular one.

Courtesy of the author

October 1978:
John celebrating at a double birthday party—his thirty-eighth and his son Sean's third—at Tavern on the Green in New York City.

Photograph by Nishi F. Saimaru, courtesy of Ms. Saimaru and the author.

December 1979:
The opening—and closing—night of Club Dakota, John's very private club (there were only three members) on the seventh floor of the building. It is perhaps the single most magical memory of my time with him.

Courtesy of the author

1980:
John and I at the Hit Factory in New York,
where he and Yoko were recording what would become
the final studio album of his life, *Double Fantasy.*

Photograph by Bob Gruen

1980:

Hard at work during the *Double Fantasy* sessions. The tin box on the console was filled with John's favorite treat—biscotti cookies.

Courtesy of the author

1980:

Yoko, John, and me in the studio.

Courtesy of the author

1984:
With Julian, Yoko, Sean, and one of Yoko's bodyguards
at the dedication of Strawberry Fields in Central Park.

Photograph by Allan Tannenbaum/Getty Images

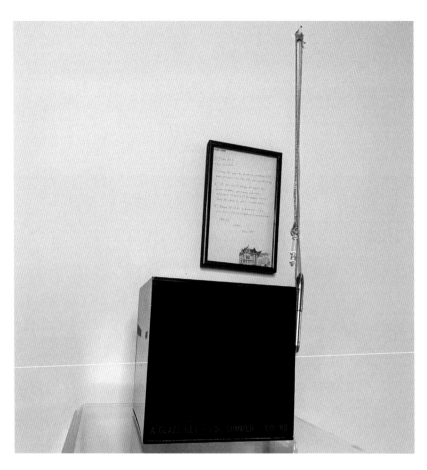

1985:

Yoko created a series of four boxes for this piece, one for each season, and kindly gifted me this summer box. The box holds a glass key, with a flashlight and instructions for viewing the art alongside it.

When the original key was broken during the Northridge earthquake of 1994, Yoko sent me a replacement key right away, which now hangs beside the box.

Courtesy of the author

FROM YOKO

A glass key
— for Summer —

1) keep the box on a south window sill and you will see the key during the day.

2) If you can't sleep at night for some reason, you may use the attached flashlight to make sure that the key is still in the box.

3) Share it with a friend — like you would of your other experiences

Enjoy!

Love,

Yoko '85

ELEVEN

Los Angeles and New York, 1974

A lot of things ended after that terrible night.

For starters, the Spector Sessions came to an abrupt halt. Once word got around about Phil firing a pistol into the ceiling, the project collapsed, and Phil did the sort of thing only Phil would think of doing: he absconded with the master tapes and held them hostage at his home. The label might have retrieved them sooner, but a few months later Phil got into a car accident and fell into a coma. Or at least that was his story; some believed the coma was just another of his over-the-top canards.

There were other hiccups—like a lawsuit by a shady, allegedly Mafia-affiliated music mogul who'd somehow finagled his way into the project—prompting the label to put the album on indefinite hold. It would, in fact, take more than a year for all the wrinkles to be ironed out and for *Rock 'n' Roll* to finally be released.

In the meantime, John's occupancy at Lou Adler's home also ended abruptly, no doubt having something to do with all the gold records John had ripped off the walls and smashed.

Instead, he and May stayed at a few locations, including a place owned by one of John's attorneys. Eventually, they moved into a beachfront mansion in Santa Monica, a 6,000-square-foot edifice that had been built in 1926 by no less a Hollywood icon than MGM cofounder Louis B. Mayer. Even more impressive to John, however, was that in the early 1960s the house had briefly been owned by Peter Lawford, who had turned it into a Rat Pack playpen, hosting wild parties and flying in Las Vegas showgirls to entertain his pals, one of whom happened to then be president of the United States.

John had a thing about JFK. A little like Phil, he found conspiracy theories fascinating; once, after listening to a radio special I had done about various assassination speculations, John tried to convince me that he had single-handedly solved the mystery. After studying the evidence, he said, it was clear to him that the driver of the presidential limousine had done it, turning around from his front seat and shooting Kennedy in the head with a pistol. No matter the mountain of evidence to the contrary—starting with the Zapruder film, in which no such thing can be seen happening—John was utterly convinced he had cracked the case.

Obviously, our friendship took a hit after the incident at

Adler's house; how could it not? For the next several months, John and I barely spent time together—at least, not in person. We would talk almost every day on the phone, as we always had, and eventually our rapport began to feel as easy and familiar as ever. But I didn't visit him at the beach house and no longer joined him for evenings at the Troubadour or the Rainbow.

Part of the reason—aside from hurt feelings needing space to heal—was that I was exceedingly busy at the time. I had my TV and radio shows to tend to, with a constant stream of interviews that kept me hopping throughout that period. (On top of hosting, I was also my own booker and researcher.) There were conversations with Raquel Welch (who invited me to her home in Beverly Hills), James Coburn (who demonstrated how he used a gong to help him meditate), Allen Ginsberg (who played the harmonium), and Jack Nicholson (whom I'd become friendly with during the Charles Manson trials; he once tagged along with me to the courthouse when I was covering them for a radio station).

There was also a particularly fascinating interview with a certain famous hypnotist, whom I would later introduce to John for what would be—by one account, anyway—a pivotal turn in the Lost Weekend chronicles. His specialty was age-regression trances, and he performed one on me during my show. In fact, he not only wound the clock back to when I was a teenager— my voice literally changed on the air—but ventured even further into my past, to a previous life in the 1800s, when I had apparently been a miner in Minnesota. Sounds unlikely, I know, but to this day part of me still believes I'm the reincarnation of an ore digger named Stephen Dworman who died in a tragic cave accident.

John, meanwhile, had shifted from the mayhem of the Spector Sessions to the slightly lesser bedlam of producing a record for his pal Harry Nilsson. The album was called *Pussy Cats*—Nilsson originally wanted to title it *Strange Pussies*, but his label put its foot down—and although its recording sessions in Burbank in the spring of 1974 never rivaled Phil's in terms of debauchery, they were more than a little unruly. John was still drinking heavily at the time, still doing cocaine, and Nilsson was never anybody's idea of a teetotaler.

The most notable thing about the *Pussy Cats* sessions, though, was who else was in the room where they happened. Ringo Starr, the only Beatle to remain consistently close to John and Yoko after the band's breakup, happened to be in L.A. and sat in on drums. When he wasn't available, the Who's Keith Moon played percussions (and, on one track, Chinese wood blocks). And although it never made it onto Nilsson's album, there was one historic moment when another ex-Beatle unexpectedly turned up at the studio and even sang with John, the first time the two of them had performed together since the Beatles split.

Enter Paul McCartney.

I can't tell you how many conversations I had with John about Paul over the years. Dozens at least, likely many more. John's feelings about his former bandmate were as complicated as they were expansive, and they changed not just from year to year but from minute to minute. Next to Yoko, Paul was the single most important relationship of John's life. They had grown up together, been teenage bandmates before the Beatles were even born, and then found themselves thrust into the biggest pop cultural phenomenon of all time, a wholly unique experience that bonded all four Beatles—but especially John and Paul, the group's front men—for life.

"I loved Paul," John declared to me. "He was me bother. I remember in the early years, before we were called the Beatles, being in the back of the van with him, going from gig to gig. And then, next thing we knew, we were in a limousine going from the airport to the Plaza Hotel the day the Beatles landed in America. You can't believe the thrill of that moment of us being together. We knew we had made it even before we did *The Ed Sullivan Show*. We knew we had conquered America.

"When we sang together," John went on, "Paul and I would share the same microphone. I'd be close enough to kiss him. Back then, I didn't wear me specs onstage—Brian Epstein said they made me look old. So we'd be playing these concerts, in front of thousands of people, but the only thing I could see was Paul's face. He was always there next to me—I could always feel his presence. It's what I remember most about those concerts.

"Paul and I had our differences early on, mostly creative ones, but we always got over them. Then I met Yoko and we fell in love. When I invited her to the recording studio during the *Let It Be* sessions, none of them took it well. This was a men's club, and no women were allowed in the recording room. But Paul seemed the most bothered about Yoko, and part of me felt it was because he was jealous. Because up till then, he had all me attention, all me love when we were recording. And now there was another. Now there was Yoko."

In the years right after the Beatles disbanded, John and Paul sometimes feuded publicly, lobbing salvos at each other in the most personal way they knew how: through their music. Paul took a swipe at John on his 1971 album, *Ram*, with a track titled "Too Many People" ("You took your lucky break and broke it in two"). A few weeks later, John recorded his bitter retort in a song called "How Do You Sleep?" ("The only thing you done was yesterday"), which ended up on his album *Imagine*. Even when they made up, it was through music. In December 1971, Paul would extend a peace offering on a Wings album called *Wild Life* with a song about John sweetly titled "Dear Friend."

But now, on March 28, 1974, John and Paul were meeting in the flesh, for the first time in ages, at a recording studio in Burbank. I wasn't present but later heard that Paul and his wife, Linda, had popped in without warning, bringing Stevie Wonder with them for some reason. According to those who were there, John and Paul seemed to pick up their friendship as if they were teenagers again, stepping out of that van to play yet another gig. When John told me about it later, I asked him how it felt, playing with his old pal. He was kind of dismissive about it, saying, "They were all just looking at us, thinking that something big was going to happen. To me, it was just playing with Paul." But peo-

WE ALL SHINE ON

ple were fascinated by the mere fact that they were in the room together, and wondered if that could be the beginning of a reunion. Which I knew better than to ask about: that just wasn't something I'd ask when I was talking to John as a friend rather than in a professional capacity.

Their reunion mini-session was never released by a label, but recordings of it eventually found their way onto a bootleg album called *A Toot and a Snore in '74*. Frankly, it's not John and Paul at their best—on one track, John can be heard offering Stevie Wonder a line of coke—but there's still something moving about hearing those two inimitable voices singing in harmony once again.

What John didn't know about that surprise encounter, though, was that, according to Yoko, Paul had an ulterior motive for the visit. A few days earlier, she had called me to explain the machinations behind the visit.

Yoko told me she spoke with Paul, who offered to speak with John.

"That's very generous," I responded. "How did you react to his offer?"

"I thought it was very kind," she said. "I was very appreciative. But I made it very clear to Paul that it wasn't something I was asking him to do. It would have to be Paul's idea, not mine, something Paul was doing on his own."

As far as Yoko was concerned, she owed John no effort at rapprochement. If he wanted to come back to her, he would have to take the initiative. He'd have to be clean and sober and prove he was ready.

To me, there was never any question that John desperately wanted to get back with Yoko. Yes, he was living with May. Yes, he had feelings for the young assistant. And yet, at some point during virtually every phone call I had with him over the long months of his Lost Weekend, John would sooner or later beseech me to talk to Yoko on his behalf. "Tell Mother I'm ready to come home, Ellie. Tell her I'm a changed man."

"I don't think she wants to hear it from me," I would say. "She wants you to show it to her."

Paul, I later heard, gave John similar advice. Sometime after popping into the studio in Burbank, he sat down with John and laid out, step by step, what he would need to do to win Yoko back. He told John he'd have to court her the way he had when they first met, to ask her on dates and bring her flowers and gifts. He'd need to clean up his act and demonstrate to Yoko that he was a complete man, whole again, capable of rebuilding their marriage. In short, he'd need to convince Yoko he was worth taking back.

It's impossible to say if Paul's presentation was what did it, or if John experienced some other epiphany around that time, but over the ensuing months he did indeed begin to clean up his act. In the summer of 1974, he started working on his next album, *Walls and Bridges*, regularly flying to New York for rehearsals and recordings at the Record Plant on West Forty-Fourth Street. By all accounts, those sessions were entirely professional, with John showing up 100 percent sober every day.

Then, as work on the album neared completion, John made a fateful decision: he decided not to wait any longer for Yoko's invitation to return to New York. Instead, towards the end of the summer, he and May rented an apartment of their own on the Upper East Side. It was a small but comfortable place that had a wraparound balcony with spectacular views of the East River. In fact, it was from that balcony, shortly after moving in, that John spotted what he believed was a UFO. I know this because he called me in L.A. immediately and asked me to find out if anybody else on the Upper East Side had seen a flying saucer rimmed with blinking lights zooming around the Manhattan skyline. (In fact, they had, at least according to the desk sergeant at a New York police precinct who was kind enough to pick up my call.)

A week or two later, I flew to New York to tape some interviews and took the opportunity to pay a visit to John and May at their new apartment—my first face-to-face meeting with John since the ugliness at Adler's house. It was an awkward encounter for numerous reasons. For one thing, I had just spent an afternoon with Yoko at the Dakota, some twenty blocks away; taking a cab across town to John and May's felt something akin to betrayal.

Making me feel even more conflicted, I couldn't get around the fact that I rather liked May. She was smart and pleasant and, in many ways, good for John. She didn't drink or smoke or do drugs, which was a major plus, particularly with John trying to dry out. She clearly put a lot of effort into taking care of him, which was no easy task. John had always required lots of taking care of. Far more importantly, she orchestrated a reconciliation between John and his estranged son, Julian, inviting the boy, then around eleven years old, to spend time with his father. For that reason alone, I gave her an enormous amount of credit.

I remember meeting Julian for the first time while John and May were living in L.A. It was an early foggy morning in Laurel Canyon, and I woke up hearing a man shouting outside my window. I recognized the voice was John's. He said, "Wake up, I want you to meet me son!" Julian was about ten years old at the time. He was an incredibly shy little boy, and somehow, I got the sense that Julian and John had been up all night together. But John was excited to keep going.

"Ellie, get dressed and come to Disneyland with us."

It was seven in the morning: at that hour, I wasn't ready for Disneyland. "John, why don't you and Julian go to Disneyland. And when you're finished, come back and we'll all have a great lunch together."

They lingered in my house for a few minutes before being driven down to Anaheim. Julian gravitated to a telescope I had in my living room. He was looking through it, playing with it, hardly speaking. I'm sure he was in an impossibly awkward position—meeting an adult who was a stranger to him, wondering why he was there.

I would not see or speak with him again until December 1980.

BUT when it came to being alone with John and May, it never felt comfortable. Perhaps sensing my apprehension, May gave me a wide berth, leaving to make some phone calls in a bedroom while John and I stood together on the balcony, catching up.

"Does this make you feel uneasy?" John asked after a beat.

"You mean being here with you and May? Yes, a little," I admitted. "It just reminds me of the fact that you and Mother are still separated, and that makes me sad."

"Well, that's the way Mother wants it," he said. "At least for now."

Then, unexpectedly, he wrapped his arm over my shoulders and added, "Don't look so glum, me boy. Put on your radio face. There's nowhere you can be that isn't where you're meant to be."

It was one of the few times he'd quoted a line to me from a Beatles song.

Walls and Bridges was released a month or so later, at the end of September 1974. John sent a prereleased signed copy ("To my little dream lover on ice, with love and old pianos," he wrote, referring to my affection for Bobby Darin's hit song), and it blew me away. I thought it contained some of John's finest solo material yet. And I wasn't the only one.

As it happened, Elton John had joined John on keyboards for one song on the album, and Elton was sure that tune was destined to become a hit. John was less certain—unlike Paul, he'd never had a No. 1 single outside of the Beatles—but Elton was so convinced, he made a bet with John. If he was right and the song was a hit, John would have to perform at Elton's upcoming concert at Madison Square Garden. John agreed, never imagining he'd have to honor that promise.

Of course, Elton was spot on: "Whatever Gets You Thru the Night" did indeed become a huge hit, John's first No. 1 solo single.

I'm aware that May has a version for how that song came to be written: she has said that John first heard its title phrase while watching a fire-and-brimstone TV preacher named Reverend Ike, who'd apparently uttered the words in one of his late-night sermons. It's possible, I suppose; as I've mentioned before, John had an affinity for TV preachers, although this one didn't seem to be his style. Reverend Ike's persistent admonition was that money was next to godliness, that Jesus wanted his followers to be rich. I didn't see John having a lot of patience for that.

I, however, had my own version for how the song may have come to be, one that involved the intervention of an even higher power than Reverend Ike: Frank Sinatra.

John and I frequently butted heads over religion. He, of course, professed to be a nonbeliever, while I had a more spiritual connection to the divine. But during one of our lengthy phone discussions on the topic—this one around the time John was preparing *Walls and Bridges*—I happened to recall a famously candid interview with Sinatra in *Playboy* magazine. At one point in that Q and A, conducted back in the early 1960s, *Playboy* asked "Ol' Blue Eyes" if he was a religious man. Sinatra's answer always stuck with me, so I shared it.

"Have you ever heard what Frank Sinatra said about religion?" I asked John.

"I don't pay much attention to what Frank Sinatra says," John answered dismissively.

"He said people should pursue whatever religion they wish to pursue. They should pray to whatever god they wanted. Sinatra said, 'I'm for anything that gets you through the night, be it prayer, tranquilizers, or a bottle of Jack Daniel's.'"

I could all but hear John mouthing Sinatra's words to himself. "I like that," he finally said out loud. "Yeah, I like that a lot."

Whatever inspired John to write the song, be it Frank or Reverend Ike or both—or neither—its ascension to the top of the charts was a turning point. John had long been jealous of Paul's post-Beatles solo success—and not just Paul's but George's, too. (Harrison had been the first of them to score a solo hit with "My Sweet Lord" in 1970.) Now, though, with "Whatever Gets You Thru the Night," he had proven to the world—and, more importantly, to himself—that he could also engineer a hit on his own. It put the old swagger back in his step, imbuing him with a renewed sense of confidence and faith in the future.

But it also meant that he owed Elton John an appearance at his upcoming concert. And it was there, in November 1974, onstage at Madison Square Garden, in front of thousands and thousands of fans, that the Lost Weekend finally began to fade to a finish.

THE details of what exactly transpired backstage that night remain, fifty years later, shrouded in some mystery. What is known is that Yoko, who'd been invited to the concert by Elton's manager, was in the audience. It's possible she knew that John would be making a surprise appearance: there had been rumors about it for days beforehand. But she certainly couldn't have been prepared for the reaction around her when Elton announced, about two-thirds into the concert, that he was bringing John onto the stage for his first public performance in two years. The crowd went berserk; the rafters literally shook. When John and Elton launched into "Whatever Gets You Thru the Night," then followed it up with "Lucy in the Sky with Diamonds" and "I Saw Her Standing There," it nearly blew the lid off the building.

After the show, Elton's manager approached Yoko and told her that Elton had requested her presence in his dressing room. He wanted to say hello before she left the arena. Yoko agreed, naturally, and was led backstage to a door with a star on it. She knocked, the entrance opened, and inside she saw her husband standing there, alone.

I cannot tell you what happened after the dressing room door closed behind them. Nobody but Yoko knows that, and she has never shared with me any details. What I can tell you is that in the weeks and months that followed, there must have been many more rendezvous as Yoko and John reestablished their connection. Perhaps John followed Paul's advice and courted his wife all over again, with flowers and dinners and gifts, even as he continued living with May in their East Side apartment.

According to one of May's early accounts, John was ultimately hypnotized into ending his relationship with her; she has long claimed that Yoko hired a mesmerist to help John quit smoking but that it was all a ruse to brainwash him into splitting up with her so he could return to Yoko. To this day, many people believe that story. But I know for certain that it wasn't true. Because, as it happens, *I'm* the one who arranged the hypnotist. Yoko had nothing to do with it.

John had remembered that I had interviewed a hypnotist on my radio show—we had talked about it on the phone a few times—and asked me if he might be able to help him kick nicotine. I called the hypnotist, planned for him to fly to New York, booked him a room in a Midtown hotel, and set up an appointment with John. In just about every respect, though, the hypnosis was a total bust. John told me immediately afterwards he was never put under; the hypnotist claimed John was but just couldn't remember. The hypnotist also turned out to be something of a diva. He disliked his hotel—he thought the desk clerks were rude—and checked out the next day, flying back to L.A. in a huff.

John didn't quit smoking, not for a minute, so it's hard to imagine the hypnotist had succeeded in brainwashing him into anything else—like, say, leaving a lover. But the very next day, John did break it off with May and returned to the Dakota, resuming his marriage to Yoko and ending, at last, the long and lonely winter that had been the Lost Weekend. He called me in L.A. shortly afterwards to share the happy news.

He said, "Let the media know the separation did not work."

PART FOUR

DOUBLE FANTASY

TWELVE

New York, 1976

Nine months after John moved back into the Dakota, Sean was born.

It was a stressful pregnancy. Yoko and John had tried to have a baby for years, but even with Hong's life-changing fertility herbs and advice, conceiving had been a struggle. The delivery had also been a harrowing ordeal: Yoko required an emergency C-section, which sent John into a furied frenzy, made even worse by the fact that most of the doctors at the hospital seemed to be more interested in shaking his hand and obtaining his autograph than tending to his wife.

Now, though, at long last, they had a son of their own, a happy, healthy, cooing little boy who happened to have been born on John's own birthday, October 9.

The numbers were clearly on their side.

I flew to New York about two weeks later to meet the newest member of the Lennon family. When I stepped off the elevator and into their apartment at the Dakota, I was greeted by the rather remarkable sight of John sitting on the all-white sofa in their all-white living room, cradling his swaddled son in his arms. Yoko was next to them, looking more peaceful and content than I'd ever seen her.

I stepped closer to get a better look at Sean, but John raised a hand to stop me.

"Now, don't get too near, Ellie," he said. "Germs, ya know."

I sat down on a white ottoman near the white piano, a respectful distance away, and just took in the scene. After the turmoil of the last couple of years, it felt to me like the Earth had finally settled into its proper axis. John and Yoko weren't just back together, where they had once belonged, but now were drawn closer than ever by the gurgling baby lying in their laps.

"Elliot, people are going to ask you if we picked October 9 as Sean's birthday to coincide with John's," Yoko said as she gently adjusted Sean's blanket. "It's not true. Because people don't decide when babies are ready to be born; babies decide that. They decide when their souls are ready to emerge and even who their parents will be." She smiled at her newborn son. "Sean is very brave to have picked us. He could have picked other people; he could have picked anyone. But he picked us."

"We considered you as his godfather," John added with a smile. "But we decided on Elton because he'd give better presents."

A short time later, an assistant arrived in the living room and carefully lifted Sean from his parents' arms for a feeding or a changing or maybe just a nap. The three of us retired to the master bedroom. They climbed onto the bed, as they so often did when we were together. I took my usual spot in the wicker chair, and John lit up a joint.

"I screwed up with me first child," he said between puffs, referring to his rough start with Julian, whom he had neglected literally since birth. During his delivery, John was playing a gig with the Beatles in East London, and just weeks later, he flew off to Barcelona for a vacation with Brian Epstein, leaving Cynthia alone to care for their newborn. "That's what a bastard I was," he said. "I just went on holiday. I was an invisible father. But I'm going to do me best this time. I'm going to devote me every waking moment to Sean. I'm going to be involved in every part of his life."

And as far as I could tell, he proceeded to do exactly that, transforming himself into the world's first—or at least most famous—househusband.

Back then, in 1975, gender roles were far more rigidly defined than they are today. Women were starting to break boundaries and claim new prerogatives as the feminist movement pushed for more sexual, economic, and political equality—but men were mostly stuck in the same old groove that had been carved out by their fathers and grandfathers. The idea of a man staying home to take care of a child while the mother went off to work seemed in those days as revolutionary as a world with no countries, no possessions, and no religion, too. It just wasn't done.

John did it anyway.

I know some people suspected that John's househusband years were some sort of PR stunt cooked up by Yoko to generate positive press. It was not. I know because, for the next six months, virtually every single phone call I had with John—and I had at least one a day—revolved around his son. He told me all about how he took Sean on walks through Central Park, carrying him in a pouch-like sleep sack on his chest, exploring the less-trodden pathways far afield from the Great Lawn. I heard endless tales about bath time—how John and Sean shared the tub together. About the VHS library John had assembled for Sean so that he wouldn't be exposed to broadcast TV advertising ("Nature videos and things like that—so that his mind can run free"). About the shelves and shelves of books John had purchased for Sean to read "when he's ready."

"John, he's only a few months old," I said, imagining stacks of J. Krishnamurti volumes piling up in Sean's nursery. "What kinds of books are you getting him?"

"Children's books!" he said. "What sort of books do ya think!"

He and Yoko obviously had plenty of help with childcare—nannies who watched after Sean like a hawk—but John was seldom far from his son's side, and it seemed to have a calming effect on his psyche. In the months after Sean's birth, I noticed something different about the timbre of John's voice on the phone: it was growing softer and gentler. He even began baking bread—and, in fact, sent me a Polaroid of one of his early loaves. John appeared to have discovered something in himself he'd always been looking for, even if he'd never been consciously aware of the search. He seemed, in the parlance of the '70s, to have "found himself."

Yoko, meanwhile, was relieved that John had so enthusiastically taken to parenting; it gave her the space to focus on running the family business, a job she was uniquely qualified to do—and that John was uniquely unqualified for and uninterested in doing. After the acrimonious dissolution of the Beatles, John never wanted to deal with another lawyer, appear for a deposition, or review another contract again. He had no idea how to handle tax matters or lien threats or leftover Beatles business or investments. I don't believe he'd ever cut a single check in his life. So he was more than happy to let Yoko take all that on herself, which she did tirelessly with skill and tenacity.

Unlike John, most of my phone conversations with Yoko around that time—and I had daily calls with her as well—seldom involved any discussion of Sean at all. Instead, she vented about journalists, gave me work assignments (like interviewing potential psychics to add to her team), occasionally read me a poem, or softly sang me a tune.

She'd say, "I've been working on two or three songs, would you like to hear them?"

I told her I'd love to, and she'd sing into the telephone very quietly. They were sweet, poetic, and somehow comforting to me. But she never recorded them—I never heard them again. She just liked to work on songs.

As it happened, I found myself flying to New York for business quite a lot in 1975 and spent more face time with John and

Yoko—and, after he was born, Sean—than I was normally accustomed to. For the most part, it was delightful. After being stress-tested to the verge of collapse by the chaos of the Lost Weekend, the bonds of our connection had never been stronger. All the sacrifices I'd made on the altar of this most unusual and exacting friendship—of living my life by the often arduous rhythms of that blinking red light on my bedroom ceiling—were finally paying off with a new sense of reciprocity. I felt more comfortable and at home with John and Yoko than I had ever felt before.

Still, if I'm to be completely frank, there were one or two moments when they drove me to the edge. For instance, there was the time I came to New York to interview Salvador Dalí, the celebrated Spanish artist and father of surrealism, famous for his paintings of melting clocks over tree branches and other works. Over a macrobiotic dinner at the Dakota, I happened to mention to John and Yoko my appointment with Dalí for the next day. Big mistake. They had met him years earlier and invited themselves to join me for the interview. As apprehensive as I was about them tagging along, there was no way I could say no, so the next morning I had my cab swing by the Dakota on my way to Dalí's grand suite at the Pierre Hotel.

Dalí, who was in his seventies at the time, was nothing if not a showman. He dressed dramatically, usually in bold double-breasted chalk-striped suits, often accompanied by a frilly ascot and silver-headed cane. He spoke flamboyantly, in an impenetrable singsong accent that seemed to me perfectly engineered to flummox radio recording equipment. Even his facial hair was dramatic, with a long, waxed mustache nearly as surreal as his art-work. I'd been looking forward to talking with him for weeks and was particularly eager to learn if his expansive imagination had at any point been fueled by experimentation with psychedelics.

Alas, the interview was a disaster, in no small part thanks to John's and Yoko's frequent interruptions. The two of them seemed oblivious to the fact that I was trying to record Dalí for a radio show. The minute he began talking about something in-teresting, John or Yoko—or both—would blurt out a comment or a joke that ruined that piece of audio. By the time I got back to my own hotel suite at the Plaza, I was completely depressed. It was the worst interview I'd ever conducted. This was my job! It'd be like me walking into a recording studio while John and Yoko were singing and blasting an air horn! Listening to the tape with a growing lump in my throat, I realized the interview was all but unusable.

I wish I could say that was the last time I let the Lennons ruin an interview, but just a short time later it happened again, when they insisted on joining me for my meeting with Baba Ram Dass, the famed psychologist, Harvard professor, and psychedelic voy-ager who helped bring Eastern philosophy into the mainstream here in the West. This time, as we huddled in Ram Dass's small apartment, Yoko insulted him by declaring, towards the end of his musings, that he sounded "a little phony." Again, I found my-self falling into a deep depression. Fortunately, the next day Ram Dass—who later became a friend—called to invite me back for a do-over. This time I didn't let John and Yoko know.

At some point around this time, my old girlfriend Louise came back into the picture, at least for a week. She'd been traveling in Europe and was returning to California by way of New York, so I offered to have her stay with me at the Plaza. It was a lovely romantic interlude, and John and Yoko once again did their (half-hearted) best to welcome her into our fold. The four of us took walks together in Central Park, dined at the Russian Tea Room, and attended the reopening of the Copacabana. But just as had been the case in Sausalito, there was a limit to how much John and Yoko would accommodate an interloper to our threesome. They picked the fellow travelers, not me. When the week was up and Louise left New York for her home in Mill Valley, I could tell they were a little more relaxed. In a sense, I was, too. I knew that Louise and I were not destined to be together. I knew a relationship with her was just another doomed cowboy dream—a dream that I had traded for a very different fantasy, one that by now had become my reality.

I believed, in a sense, that I was married to John and Yoko.

And then, one Thursday night in February 1976, as I was dining with a friend in West Hollywood, I received a piece of news that shattered my carefully curated life into a thousand nightmarish pieces. A waiter brought a phone to our table, and I learned from the voice on the other end that Sal Mineo had been murdered.

Let's rewind here for a few words about Sal. When I, as a young broadcasting student at City College, first encountered him in 1962, he was hovering near the top of the Hollywood food chain. He had started out as a child actor, landing a bit part as one of the kids in the Broadway production of *The King and I*. But by the time he was sixteen, he was already climbing the ladder to movie stardom, starting with his Oscar-nominated gig opposite James Dean in 1955's *Rebel Without a Cause*. From then on, it was one plum part after another, with roles in 1956's *Giant*, 1957's *Dino*, 1958's *Tonka*, 1959's *The Gene Krupa Story*, 1960's *Exodus*, and 1962's *The Longest Day* and *Escape from Zahrain*. By the time he'd turned twenty-one, Sal was earning upwards of $200,000 a picture, a huge sum in those days.

Naturally, being only twenty-one, he ended up spending almost all of it.

For a while he rented a bachelor pad up in the Hollywood Hills; he'd park his motorcycle in the living room. Later he bought a used Bentley and moved to a beach house in Santa Monica not far from the one Peter Lawford had once owned. The parties Sal threw there in the early 1960s were epic bacchanals that must have made Lawford's look like backyard barbecues. There were never-ending caviar buffets and free-flowing champagne—Sal blew a good chunk of his earnings on both—and sometimes even live entertainment. Some of the most famous actors and musicians of the era became regular attendees: I remember rubbing elbows with Jane Fonda, Lee Remick, Roddy McDowall, Eva Marie Saint, and scores of others. At one party, Sal introduced me to a teenage boy who had sung a few numbers for the gilded crowd, who all fell in love with him. Sal told me he was managing the teen and had helped land him a spot on a music show called *Shindig!* His name was Bobby Sherman, and he went on to become a heartthrob for a time.

Again, I have no understanding of why Sal took to me, but he did. As I've previously shared, it's the story of my life, being befriended by the fabled and adored. But after we met at that nightclub on the Sunset Strip where I'd gone to interview a stage hypnotist for my college radio station, we became good pals. He put me up when I was looking for work, took a genuine interest in my fledgling career, went out of his way to make room for me in his life. At one point, while he was shooting the biblical epic *The Greatest Story Ever Told*—he played Uriah, a soldier in the army of King David—he invited me to the desert set in Moab, Utah, to spend a few days watching him act in the extravagant production. It was a gesture of pure friendship and kindheartedness. He had no motive other than to make me happy.

Although we were close, I had no idea that Sal was bisexual. He was engaged at the time to the British actress Jill Haworth, whom he'd met on the set of *Exodus*, and they seemed to me to be very much in love. In fact, they appeared together on the cover of *Life* magazine in 1960, the literal picture of a happy Hollywood couple. Whatever secret life Sal might have been living—and in those days, that kind of secret could destroy a career—he never shared any of the details with me. In retrospect, I suppose his penchant for leather biker gear might have been a clue, but I guess I was naïve. I just thought it was a sartorial hangover from his *Rebel Without a Cause* days.

In any case, Sal made some excellent films through the '60s—

Who Killed Teddy Bear was one of my personal favorites—but by the end of the decade, as he entered his thirties, the roles began to dry up, and so did his money. Having saved almost nothing, he traded in his Bentley for a Chevrolet Chevelle and eventually ended up moving to a dreary one-bedroom apartment in West Hollywood, on Holloway Drive, just below the Sunset Strip. He survived with TV guest spots on shows like *Hawaii Five-O, My Three Sons,* and *Columbo.* His last big screen role was in 1971, as Dr. Milo, a talking chimp in *Escape from the Planet of the Apes.* For a while he coasted on the fumes of his fame, but even that currency ultimately ran out. I remember in 1974, or maybe 1975, having dinner with him at a bistro near Sunset Plaza Drive, a regular watering hole frequented by actors and actresses. When the server brought him the bill, he tried to add it to his tab. The waiter politely declined and asked for a credit card, noting that Sal had already accrued a sizable debt. Sal was outraged.

"Do you know how many people I've brought to this restaurant?" he bellowed, throwing his napkin onto the table. "This is an insult! How dare you!"

That was one of the last times I remember seeing him alive. And now, in February of 1976, at a different restaurant in West Hollywood, I was trying to process the news, delivered between courses, that Sal was gone. And not merely dead but murdered. Stabbed to death in a brutal and senseless random slaying.

I quickly left the restaurant and drove to Sal's apartment, the scene of the crime. Later I'd learn that he'd been killed after returning from a play rehearsal and parking his Chevelle in his car port. The assailant had jumped out of the bushes, stabbed him once in the heart, grabbed his wallet, and made away with a grand total of $11. There were police cars everywhere, their cherry lights casting a riot of sickening colors over the palm trees lining the street. About a hundred yards away, lying in the driveway, covered by some sort of yellow tarp, was my friend's dead body.

I don't remember how long I stood there watching—it may have been minutes; it may have been longer—but eventually I found my way back to Laurel Canyon. My telephone messaging service had collected dozens of calls from friends and reporters who'd heard about the murder, but also a few from a homicide detective who wanted to talk to me. I returned that call first, and within minutes, a couple of officers were knocking on my door. They interviewed me for a very long time, asking me about Sal's private life, about our friendship, about my whereabouts during the evening. It dawned on me that at this early stage of what would turn out to be a two-year investigation—ultimately resulting in the arrest and conviction of a twentysomething gang member who already had a long rap sheet stretching back years—I was what they'd call today a "person of interest." I didn't take it personally. As far as the police were concerned, at that point anyone who knew Sal was a suspect. The next day, I drove to the police station and took a polygraph test to clear my name.

At the request of Sal's brother, I ended up arranging to have Sal's body flown across the country for burial in suburban Mamaroneck, New York, where Sal's family lived. Of course, I was on the flight escorting my friend's remains. But I didn't go alone. Sal had also been close to David Cassidy—the two shared the common bond of being teen idols—and David volunteered to join me on the grim crossing. It was, to put it mildly, a difficult trip, made even more grueling by how David dealt with his own grief. We started out sharing stories about Sal, which was somewhat cathartic and helpful. But as the flight dragged on, David began to drink heavily and would take frequent bathroom breaks, returning to his seat full of nervous, coke-fueled energy.

As terrible as the journey was, though, what was to follow on the ground in New York was so much worse.

The funeral—which David didn't attend, fearful that his presence would create a media frenzy—was beyond brutal. I suppose all of them are, but at that point in my life I had never experienced real grief. The closest I'd ever come—and, truly, it wasn't remotely close at all—was when my dog Shane became terminally ill and I had to put him down. Again, it's not a relevant comparison—a dog is obviously not a person—but at that point in my life it was the only comparison I had. Sal's death, of course, was a whole different manner of suffering.

When the services were finally over and Sal was laid to rest in Mamaroneck, I took a car service back to the city and checked in at the Plaza, hoping to finally get some rest. But along with my room key, the clerk at the front desk handed me a stack of pink phone message slips, many of them from John and Yoko, asking me to come to the Dakota as soon as I arrived.

I decided John and Yoko would have to wait and headed to

the elevators. The minute I opened my hotel room door, though, the phone rang.

"Ellie, Mother and I want to see you," John said.

"John, I'm burnt out and completely exhausted. Can we visit tomorrow?"

"Mother and I would really like to see you now," he repeated.

I was too tired to argue, so I put down the phone and, without changing out of my funeral suit, returned to the hotel lobby and grabbed a cab. A few minutes later, I was on the seventh floor of the Dakota, about to enter John and Yoko's apartment. Before stepping through the anteroom door, though, I noticed something new dangling from its brass knob: a small strand of Tibetan bells and beads, which I recognized as mystical totems that were supposed to possess magical protective powers. I guessed they'd been added when Sean joined the family. They made a sweet tinkling sound when I pushed open the door.

John gave me a bear hug as soon as he saw me, then led me to the kitchen, where Yoko was waiting. She, too, put her arms around me; it was one of the few times she'd volunteered a physical embrace. We sat at their kitchen table, and I was surprised to see a bottle of Chardonnay waiting for me with a single glass; for obvious reasons, Yoko normally kept their home an alcohol-free zone. Not for the first time that day, I burst into tears.

We talked for hours, well into the night. I was exhausted and emotionally depleted, but something strange started to happen the more we spoke. Miraculously, I began to feel better. I was still grief-stricken, of course—shattered—but gradually I could feel the despair slowly lifting. I was where I needed to be, with the people I needed to be with, hearing the voices I needed to hear. I was with family.

"Tell me how you are feeling," Yoko asked softly.

"Completely empty," I answered.

"Sometimes, when someone we love dies, we feel abandoned. Do you feel abandoned?" she asked.

"Yeah, I think that's a good word for it."

"But you're not alone, Elliot. You're here. With people who love you."

John smiled. But he seemed to be curious about Sal's murder and couldn't resist asking questions.

"Did Sal know this man, Ellie?"

"The police don't have any of those answers, but it appears it was a random act of violence," I said. "It seems Sal didn't know the man."

"It could happen to anybody or everybody," John said.

"Do you ever worry it could happen to you?" I asked.

"If it could happen to anybody or everybody, why would I waste any time worrying about it happening to me?"

"But you never have bodyguards or security people around you. I've been wondering about that since we first met. Why don't you protect yourselves?"

"All me life I've had guys around me who were supposed to be protecting me. When the group toured, there were hundreds of police around us. But if they want to get you, they're gonna get you. They could get you in Disneyland. Look at all the people that Kennedy had around him. I don't need bodyguards. I don't want them. I'm just a rock 'n' roll singer."

"But John," I pressed, "Don't you think having more people around you—or just one more—would make you even slightly more safe?"

"No," he answered. "Even the thought of it makes me cringe." He paused a moment.

"I've never been afraid of death," he added after a beat. "To me, it's like getting out of one car and into another."

Yoko nodded in agreement. "Nothing can be prevented if it's destined to happen," she said. "We once had a session with one of the best palm readers in Greece and she said that John would be killed on an island. Should we avoid all islands? Should we never go anywhere? If it is going to happen, it is going to happen."

I realized there was nothing I could say to alter their positions.

As comforting as John and Yoko were, my exhaustion began to overtake me. I needed some sleep. So, as the sun started to come up over the island of Manhattan, Yoko granted me another semi-hug as John walked me to their door. When he opened it to let me out, we heard the tiny Tibetan bells jingling.

"This," John said, pointing to the magical totems hanging from the doorknob, "this is all the protection we need."

THIRTEEN

Japan, 1977

One sweltering afternoon in the summer of 1977, a courier on a motorbike turned up at my house in Laurel Canyon. I wasn't expecting a delivery, so I was a little puzzled when he handed over a large manila envelope. Inside was a first-class airline ticket to Tokyo and a note in John's unmistakable handwriting.

"We miss you," it read. "Come join us."

John and Yoko, along with now nearly two-year-old Sean, had departed for Japan a few months earlier for a long sojourn in Yoko's homeland. Her family had property outside of Tokyo, in the small village of Karuizawa, where the Lennons had taken up residence in a beautiful old hotel called the Mampei. Although our daily phone calls stopped while they were away—the red light on my bedroom ceiling remained eerily unblinking for weeks on end—I received over a hundred letters and postcards from their travels filled with John's inimitable doodles and quirky, pun-filled wordplay. After years of almost daily telephone calls, the letters and postcards were a refreshing and fun way to feel connected to my dear friends, and I enjoyed every one.

Still, I missed them, and, as it happened, the invitation couldn't have arrived at a more opportune moment. I'd been working in radio for more than a decade—engaging in what would amount to hundreds of hours of broadcasting—and was at that point starting to feel burnt out from the endless, stressful cycle of finding talent, booking talent, and then endeavoring to engage that talent in scintillating on-air conversation. I was ready for a change, contemplating a career switch—the brave new world of media consulting sounded potentially promising—and had just weeks earlier taken a break from my regular programming. For the first time since hopping into the Dragon Wagon for that road trip to San Francisco, I had a stretch of empty days on my calendar. Why *not* spend some of them in Japan?

So, about a week later, I was packing my bags and preparing for my first-ever trans-Pacific flight the following morning. To keep myself company as I folded my favorite Hawaiian shirts into my suitcase, I switched on the TV. That's when I heard something over the airwaves that suddenly made me stop packing.

Elvis Presley had died.

Obviously, it wasn't as devastating to me as Sal's death the year before. I had never even met Elvis. Still, he'd been a huge part of my cultural evolution, far more important to me than even the Beatles. To me and to countless other teenagers of my generation, Presley represented freedom and rebellion. We'd never seen anyone who looked like him, sang like him, and especially moved like him. He was the James Dean of rock music: defiant, original, and dangerous.

I knew Elvis had been a hugely influential figure to John as well. Without Presley, it's entirely possible that John might never have picked up a guitar and the Beatles might never have existed. "Before Elvis," John once famously said, neatly summing up Presley's importance to rock 'n' roll, "there was nothing."

Phone calls across the Pacific in those days were not commonplace, but I wanted to be the one to break the news to John. I assumed he'd be upset and might need to talk about it; I wanted to be there for him, if only by phone, to reciprocate the attention he and Yoko had bestowed on me after Sal's funeral. So I placed a call to Karuizawa.

"I was just thinking about you!" John said, sounding chipper. Clearly, word of Elvis's death had not yet reached him.

"Look, John, I have some bad news."

"What is it, then?" he said, his tone suddenly serious.

"It was just announced that Elvis has died."

"What happened? How'd he die?"

"They're saying it was a massive heart attack."

He paused for a very long time. Then he did something I'll never forget, something that stunned me a little. He was flippant.

"Elvis died when he went into the Army," he said.

There was another pause, with trans-Pacific static filling the line for a good ten seconds. "The difference between the Beatles and Elvis is that Elvis died and his manager is still alive," he finally said. "But with the Beatles the manager died and we're still alive. But I never wanted to be a forty-year-old bloke who died singing his golden hits in a jumpsuit in Las Vegas."

I didn't know how to respond, so I didn't say anything.

"Send two white gardenias to his grave," he continued, softening a bit at my silence. "With a note that says, 'Rest in peace, John and Yoko.'"

"Okay."

"See you soon, then?"

"Yes," I said, a little shaken. "See you in Japan."

I remember thinking in that moment that someday, years from then, a reporter might ask me what John Lennon had said when I told him Elvis had died. And I knew how much I would want to resist answering that question truthfully.

In my shock about Elvis's death and rush to comfort John, I'd forgotten how complicated his feelings were towards Presley. Somewhere along the line, John's teenage admiration of Elvis had curdled into disappointment—and I knew exactly when that started to happen. In the mid-1960s, at the height of Beatlemania, John and his bandmates met Elvis at his home in Bel Air, and it did not go well. John kept asking Presley why he'd made all those "terrible movies"—*Viva Las Vegas* had just come out—which naturally set Elvis on edge. He disliked John immediately. Later, as John became more political, speaking out against the war in Vietnam, incurring Nixon's wrath and the subsequent threats of deportation, John grew equally contemptuous of his old idol. Presley, after all, had been a huge Nixon supporter and had even gone to the White House to receive an honorary federal narcotics agent badge.

The next morning I settled in for the eleven-hour flight to Tokyo. I'd never been to Asia before and was excited about the adventure ahead, but also a little nervous. Karuizawa was not exactly a popular tourist destination, and it was complicated to get there. John and Yoko had sent ahead extremely specific instructions for what to do when I landed: a man would meet me at the airport and take me to a railroad station, where I'd board a train and get off at the eleventh stop, then another man would meet me with further instructions. It all reminded me of the first time we had met, the wild-goose chase in Ojai. But this time I was worried, not without good reason, that I might find myself lost in a land where I didn't speak a word of the native language.

Sure enough, after we landed, I couldn't find the man who was supposed to meet me at the airport—at least, not at first. After wandering around my arrival gate for I have no idea how long, I eventually spotted a Japanese man in a jacket and tie who appeared to be waiting for someone, presumably me. This, thankfully, turned out to be my first Karuizawa connection. He didn't speak English, but after some hand signaling we did indeed end up at a rail station, where he deposited me on what I prayed was the correct train.

As instructed, I got off at the eleventh stop. By this time it was about three in the morning, and the station was completely deserted except for an elderly man with a long gray beard waiting by a pair of broken-down bicycles. I smiled at him and said, "John Lennon?" He smiled back and bowed. I tried again. "Yoko Ono?" I asked. This time his face lit up; I obviously had the right man. He also didn't speak English but somehow managed to convey that we were to bicycle to the Mampei; my bags would follow later. Apparently, in these parts, bicycles were the dominant mode of transportation.

As it turned out, it was a marathon ride, at least six or seven miles. There were several moments when I was pretty sure I was going to have a coronary. And then, of course, it started raining. But finally, after about forty minutes, I spotted some gardens in the distance. Then, as we pedaled closer, I saw the Mampei, a charming old inn opened in 1902—when Japan was first starting to cultivate Western tourism—that looked a bit like an alpine retreat transplanted from a Swiss mountainside. As we rolled up to the hotel's stately entrance, the intoxicating scent of cherry blossoms nearly lifted me off my bike.

I turned around to give the old man a tip, but he had already vanished. Instead, I found myself standing next to a lovely young Japanese woman who silently led me through a shoji door and into the hotel, where, after a minute or two of filling out paperwork, I was escorted to the inn's mineral baths. After the flight from L.A. and the train and bike rides, soaking in these magic waters was one of the most relaxing experiences of my life. Afterwards, I was given a kimono and led to my room, which was filled with exotic flowers and pounds of fresh fruit. There was also a note from John and Yoko.

"We're all together now, just like family," it read. "We'll see you in the morning."

My lifelong insomnia was no match for the 5,500-mile journey from Los Angeles to Karuizawa and I fell asleep almost as soon as my head hit the tatami mat. I don't often dream, or at least I don't often remember when I do, but that night I dreamt about being on a small boat—more of a raft, really—with John and Yoko. We were floating on a lake as still and calm as the Mampei's mineral baths, and occasionally Yoko would reach down and pull a fish from the water, talk to it in Japanese, and set it free. Then John dove in for a swim and disappeared under the raft. When he didn't resurface, I began to panic; I did not know how to swim, so I couldn't rescue him. But Yoko gently touched my arm and said, "It's okay, Elliot, John will be back when he's ready."

I had no idea what the dream meant, if anything, but when I was startled awake the next day by a knocking on my door, I was extremely relieved to see John and Yoko standing there, safe and sound, him in a beautiful antique kimono, her in a white silk robe. Indeed, the two of them had never looked healthier. Over the two months they'd been in Japan, they'd radically altered their lifestyle—particularly John, who in New York considered chocolate cake one of the basic food groups. They were eating fresh fruits and vegetables and plenty of fresh fish, were bicycling everywhere, and were leaner and fitter than I'd ever seen them.

They both had shimmering long hair—something about the enchanted water here gave their locks a nearly surreal sheen—and their skin appeared almost to glow. They seemed to me like a vision, almost as if I were still dreaming.

After we embraced each other—more of a pat on the back with Yoko—they took me for a stroll along a nearby lane, where we stopped for a sushi lunch. I should note here that sushi in Karuizawa was not the same thing as sushi in Los Angeles. The fish in this town were literally plucked out of an eight-hundred-year-old stream running next to the restaurant and served so fresh, you could feel them wiggling down your throat.

Every day was a new adventure. One morning we cycled up a hill to a tea shop, maybe five or six miles away. Yoko always rode ahead, and John and I would have to struggle to catch our breath as we tried to meet her. Yoko went out of her way to try to find experiences that would be unique and special for me—it was one of her ways of inviting me in, showing her warmth. Although, some of them were a bit too much for me. Yoko took us to a restaurant that served turtle soup. It was similar to going to a restaurant where you pick your lobster from a tank, but in this case, they'd bring out the turtle for turtle soup and dangle it in front of you. A few minutes later, it would come back, the soup in the shell with the turtle's feet in it. I didn't opt for seconds.

"So," I asked over a later, turtle-free lunch, "what else have you two been doing here? How do you usually spend your days when you're not hosting me?"

They both looked at me as if I'd arrived from another planet.

"Well," John answered, "we're just *being*."

"Just being?"

"After you slow down for a while, you'll understand," Yoko answered.

She was right. And it didn't take long. After a few days, I noticed that time moved at a far more leisurely pace in Karuizawa. It might have been because there was less sensory input than in New York or Los Angeles—no honking cars, no bustling crowds. Just the soft sound of shakuhachi music wafting through the air, making the days seem to drift along like tangerine dreams on marmalade clouds. There might be yoga in the morning, or a stroll with Sean, or bike rides up the hill to an espresso café that John and Yoko had discovered. One afternoon Yoko arranged for John and me to get massages at a Shinto monastery where an order of elderly blind women used mystical tactile techniques to transfer healing energy. It was an amazing, magical place—a hundred years earlier, it had been a sanctuary for battered Japanese wives—and I left feeling as if I had truly been touched by something preternatural.

At one point we took a trip to Kyoto, about a five-hour drive from Karuizawa, to visit some of the ancient Shinto temples. Surprisingly, John was the one most enthralled by the experience, closing his eyes and clasping his hands in prayer as he bent before the shrines. Ironically, the man who had written "God," a song proclaiming nonbelief in pretty much everything having to do with religion, got so wrapped up in Shinto ritual, even Yoko took notice. I recall at one temple there was a place where people could purchase fortunes on small pieces of paper and hang them on strings as offerings to the spirit world. John and Yoko and I all chose our notes and hung them up.

John bowed his head and closed his eyes.

Later I half-teasingly asked him, "What did you pray for?"

"It wasn't a prayer," he answered defensively. "It was just a wish. I wished for peace. What did you wish with yours?"

"I asked that the spirits bless us all," I answered.

"Ah, well then, you totally missed the point, mate," he said. "The spirit is in you."

As blissful as our stay in Karuizawa was, John and Yoko had been there quite a while before I joined them. So, a few weeks after I arrived, when Yoko's psychic advisors determined that the time was ripe for the Lennons to move on, they decided to decamp for Tokyo, where Yoko had business meetings and family get-togethers. We all packed our bags and headed for the railroad station in Kyoto, where we boarded the then relatively new bullet train, the fastest, most luxurious way to travel in Japan without leaving the ground. As the name implies, it wasn't a long journey—at 180 miles per hour, the trip took only about two and a half hours—but Yoko, who'd been our nonstop translator, tour guide, and entertainment director during our weeks in Karuizawa, decided to use that time for a well-deserved nap, leaving John and me alone to entertain each other.

"Do you want to play a meaningless game?" I asked John as the train whooshed past the blurry Japanese countryside.

"If it's meaningless, why would I want to play it?" he asked.

"Because it makes the time go away," I answered.

"Nothing makes time go away," he said. "But what's your meaningless game, then?"

What I had in mind was a variation of Geography. In that game, one person names a city, country, or continent and the next person has to come up with a location that begins with the last letter of the place that's just been named. So, if I said New York, the other person would have to think up a city that began with the letter *K*, like Kandahar, and then I'd have to name a city that began with the letter *R*, like Rio de Janeiro, and so on. Only, in the version I wanted to play with John, instead of cities, we were going to use Beatles songs.

"Beatles songs?" John asked. "That's really what you want to do on the train?"

"Yeah. I think it could be fun."

"I never think about Beatles songs," he said. "I use them as me calendar. That's how I remember when things in me life happened: I remember where I was when Paul and I wrote a song. But outside of that, I don't give them much attention. I seldom play them. I rarely listen to them. Especially the early songs. It's a daft game."

"Let's try it anyway," I pressed on. "Part of the idea of this sort of game is that it takes you out of the intellectual process. It occupies the mind but in a nonintellectual way."

"Well, you're very good at taking me out of the intellectual process, because this is a really pointless game. Do you have a better one?"

"No," I said. "I don't."

And so, while zooming through Japan on the fastest train in the world, we played the Beatles song game.

John was terrible at it. I named "Come Together," and he got stuck trying to think of a Beatles song that began with the letter *R* ("Revolution," "Rocky Raccoon," and "Run for Your Life" come to mind). I named "A Day in the Life," and for whatever reason he was unable to think of "Eleanor Rigby" or "Eight Days a Week." After about five minutes, I could see his frustration mounting.

"What are you trying to prove, Ellie?" he fumed. "I don't know why you brought up this game. I've spent me whole life trying not to play games."

"Is your frustration perhaps due to the fact that you can't name a Beatles song that begins with the letter *D*?"

I had just named "I Want to Hold Your Hand," and John had been unable to come up with "Day Tripper," "Dear Prudence," or "Drive My Car."

"Why are you trying to provoke me?" John nearly shouted.

"It's just a game," I said. "It's supposed to be fun."

"It's a stupid game," he sneered, then pulled his hat over his forehead, leaned back, and pretended to fall asleep.

In Tokyo, we stayed at the Okura, which at the time was the poshest hotel in the city, the Japanese equivalent of the Plaza in

New York. And by "stayed" I mean we almost never left the premises, as per Yoko's explicit instructions. She had good reasons for wanting John to remain inside.

For starters, Tokyo was—and still is—one of the most complicated, easy-to-get-lost-in cities on earth. Even lifelong residents find its byzantine web of alleys and passageways confounding. For another, unlike Karuizawa, where John may have stood out as a gaijin tourist but was seldom recognized as a former Beatle, Tokyo was not a safe place for him to be wandering the streets. Even back in 1977, the city was bursting with a cosmopolitan population of more than 27 million, a large portion of which would certainly recognize a former Beatle when they saw one. One of the reasons Yoko had chosen the Okura was that it boasted exceptional internal security. She knew John would be safe there, provided he didn't wander beyond its protective moat.

Fortunately, the Okura was enormous, a small city of its own. And the Lennons had reserved the presidential suite, which was itself so huge, one might easily get lost in it. The living room was so big, John and Sean sometimes played soccer in it when they weren't racing in toy pedal cars down its seemingly endless hallways. If we had stayed in Tokyo for only a few days or even a week, restricting our movements to the Okura might not have been much of a problem. John was used to being holed up in hotels. For years, he'd literally lived in them. (The Beatles had performed more than 1,400 concerts around the world during their time together.) But we ended up lingering there much longer because Yoko's advisors were having a hard time finding safe travel dates. After a couple of weeks, John began to grow restless and moody. One night, while Yoko was out and Sean had been put to bed by the nanny, John sat in the enormous living room lazily strumming his acoustic guitar, talking to me about how bored and homesick he was.

"I just want to be in me own bed with me Scott amp and me books," he said.

"Yeah," I responded. "I hope the numbers will be favorable soon so we can leave."

John's plucking on his guitar morphed into a recognizable tune—he started playing "Jealous Guy"—when all of a sudden the elevator that led from the lobby directly to the presidential suite swooshed open. A Japanese couple, dressed for dinner, stepped out, strolled around, took in the living room's spectacular view of the city, then sat down on one of the couches. John and I just looked at each other. Obviously, the couple had taken a forbidden turn into the wrong elevator. How this happened, we never did figure out; it was obviously a shocking breach of security. But the couple must have assumed they'd found the hotel's penthouse cocktail lounge: it was, after all, an expansive sofa-lined space with live entertainment. They lit a couple of cigarettes and glanced around for a waitress to take their drink orders. John and I grinned at each other, and he kept playing. After a few more smokes, the couple got up and, looking annoyed and disappointed, headed back down the elevator to search for a more exciting club.

And so it came to pass that John Lennon's final public concert would be held in a hotel room in Tokyo for a couple of Japanese strangers who obviously had no idea who he was. Fate does indeed have a wicked sense of humor.

A few evenings later, when Yoko was out again visiting with family, John decided he'd had enough of being cooped up. "I want to go outside," he announced. "I want fresh air. We've been stuck in this bloody hotel for weeks."

"Mother told us not to leave," I reminded him. "We don't have any security and we don't know our way around the city." I sensed a rebellion was brewing.

"I know what Mother said," he went on. "I want to go out."

We were like two brothers arguing over whether to defy a parent's instructions and do something dangerous without adult supervision. But John was the older sibling, even if I tended to be the more cautious one, and it was impossible not to follow his lead. I wasn't about to block the elevator door.

It was just after sunset when we left the hotel and took a cab into the heart of Tokyo, which was every bit as shambolic and confusing as Yoko had warned. We were instantly dazed by a jumble of flashing neon and knocked about by massive waves of shoulder-to-shoulder foot traffic. I'd never seen a more congested city; it was like Times Square squared. But John just bounded ahead, fearless as always, taking in the sights. He seemed particularly interested in the sake bars that dotted every block. I dreaded what was coming.

"I want sake," he said.

"Are you sure that's a good idea?" I implored, thinking of

Yoko's post–Lost Weekend admonitions that at all costs I should keep John away from alcohol. She knew, as did I, that John became a very different person when he drank.

"It's just sake!" he said as he headed into one of the lounges. "It's like having a glass of wine." I followed close behind as we inched our way to the crowded bar. He was about to order when he realized he had no money. He never had money. He nudged my shoulder and told me to get him a sake. I searched my pockets and fished out some crumpled Japanese bills. Against my better judgment, I ordered one sake for John and one glass of white wine for myself, which took all of fifteen seconds to appear in front of us. I had barely reached for my wineglass when John smacked his empty sake cup back down on the bar. "Order another," he commanded.

I was in too deep now; there was no way of talking him out of it. So I ordered another sake, then another, then another. But as John downed his fourth drink, I began to notice a familiar energy pattern forming in the bar. I obviously didn't speak Japanese, but I heard a growing hum of murmurs, then someone loudly said the word "Beatle" and then somebody else said "John" and suddenly the already jam-packed room felt even more crowded as people pushed closer to us, their drinks sloppily spilling onto their sleeves.

"John," I said, "we better get out of here. It could get rough."

He downed the rest of his sake and we moved towards the door. But by now he'd been recognized, and half the bar filed out with us, following us down the street. Within minutes, virtually everyone on the sidewalk had somehow been made aware that John Lennon was in their midst. Scores of pedestrians began swarming around us, thrusting pens at John, shouting in Japanese and demanding autographs.

"We've got to get out of here," I shouted over the din. "This isn't safe. I'm hailing a cab."

John just glowered at me, the alcohol already activating the Mr. Hyde side of his personality. "I want another sake," he said through gritted teeth, ignoring the fan riot erupting around him. "I'm not asking; I'm bloody telling."

"John, this is dangerous! There's a lot of plate glass windows on these buildings. Somebody could get hurt. *You* could get hurt."

That's when he grabbed me by my lapels and pushed me back against a concrete wall. "If I want to have a fucking drink, you're not standing in my way!" he shouted. "You got that?"

But, of course, there was no way for John to get another drink. Even in his drunken state, he could see the crowd was out of control, that it wasn't going to let him simply slip into a different sake bar. His only choice was to climb into the cab that I managed to catch and return to his suite at the Okura, where Yoko was waiting, looking very much like a furious parent. I could tell from the expression on her face there would be consequences. Maybe not for John, but certainly for his supposedly more sensible younger sibling.

"I'm very, very disappointed in you," Yoko said, scolding me in the living room after John sheepishly slunk off to the bedroom to sleep off the sake. "Many times I told you not to let John drink alcohol. Many times I told you not to let him leave the hotel. Why did you disobey me? Why did you ignore my wishes?"

"I'm very sorry, Yoko," I said, studying my shoelaces, resisting the urge to argue that there was no way of stopping it, and that while I didn't agree with all of John's decisions, he was still an adult, beyond my control. "I will not make this mistake again."

The next day, John awkwardly approached me. "How'd it go with Mother?" he asked.

"She expressed her disappointment in me," I said, "for allowing last night to happen."

"I figured she would blame you," he said. "She didn't say anything to me. Sorry, Ellie."

It was perhaps not coincidental that soon after this escapade Yoko decided it was time to return to America. Her advisors still calculated that it was unsafe for John to fly directly from Tokyo to New York, but Yoko came up with an astrologically acceptable alternative. She would fly directly from Tokyo to New York, while John and I—along with Sean and his nanny—would fly to Hong Kong. Then the nanny and Sean would fly from Hong Kong to New York, while John and I would return via a more circuitous route, traveling to Bangkok to Dubai to Frankfurt, and finally arriving in New York nearly two days later.

John and Yoko always flew in the front of the plane. Indeed, they not only purchased first-class tickets for themselves but bought the seats adjacent to them as well, keeping them empty so that John would never find himself sitting next to a stranger having to explain why the Beatles weren't getting back together. Once the new 747 double-decker jets were introduced, it was not uncommon for them to splurge on the entire upstairs cabin. They'd done just that on the way to Japan, so that Sean could lay out his toy train tracks and spend the flight playing on the floor.

In some ways, they were very different sorts of travelers. Yoko was the type to pack twenty-five suitcases, leaving nothing she might want behind. John, on the other hand, took enormous pride in being able carry all the essentials he'd need for a journey around the globe in a single attaché case. He adored attaché cases and owned dozens of them, many of which he'd purchased from the duty-free catalogues he'd find in airplane seat pockets. But when it came to the details of their itineraries—when and where to fly—John left those decisions entirely to his wife and her advisors, even if it meant schlepping the wrong way around the world for two days. I never heard him once complain about Yoko's sometimes tortuous travel agenting.

There were, however, occasional hiccups. For instance, while our flights to Hong Kong and Dubai went off without a hitch, John and I did run into some trouble in Frankfurt, Germany— John's first trip to that country since 1966, and only his second since 1962, when the Beatles played the Star-Club in Hamburg's notorious red-light district. Somehow, the desk clerk at the airport hotel couldn't find our reservations, and no amount of my pleading could convince him to give us some rooms. I reported the bad news to John, who'd been "hiding" in the hotel lobby by using his old disguise of staring close up at a wall.

"They have no rooms," I said.

"They have rooms!" he said. "They always have rooms!"

"Maybe you can try?" I asked. "I mean, you are John Lennon. If anybody can get us rooms, you can."

"I can't do that," he said. "I can't say, 'I'm a Beatle: give us rooms.'"

"John, it's raining outside. We can't walk around Frankfurt in the rain all night."

John sighed and headed towards the front desk to reluctantly play the Beatle card. For the next few minutes, I watched as he and the clerk chatted, occasionally smiled, and at one point even laughed. And then, for some reason, John pointed at me. The clerk stared in my direction, nodding furiously. A few moments later, John came over with two keys.

"I told him you were Paul McCartney," John said. "That seemed to work."

It worked, all right. I was given a gorgeous suite with a feather bed and a sauna. A little later, the desk manager sent up a tray of delicious snacks and a bottle of wine. Life as Paul McCartney was clearly good.

But then, early in the morning, John was at my door, looking tired and miserable. "I couldn't sleep," he said. "This place is such a dive. They gave me a bloody closet."

"What do you mean?" I asked. "This place is great!"

John stepped into the suite, surveyed its opulence, and his jaw practically hit the floor.

"I guess the desk manager liked the fact that I wrote 'Yesterday,'" I joked.

John didn't laugh.

SOME twelve hours later, we found ourselves in the upper deck of a jumbo jet making its descent into John F. Kennedy International Airport. After so much time in Japan and then so many hours in the air, it felt a little surreal to finally land back in the United States. Hustling through immigration, it occurred to me that this must have been an especially sweet moment for John. Japan had been his first overseas excursion since his immigration victory finally granting him permanent residence in the United States. For the first time in years, he didn't have to worry about being turned away at the border. On the contrary, getting his passport stamped at JFK may well have been the high point of his whole trip. The agent at the customs booth examined his documents, smiled, then said the words John had so fervently yearned to hear for so long.

"Welcome home, Mr. Lennon."

FOURTEEN

The Dakota, 1979 to 1980

I don't know how they got ahold of it. I never asked; they never told. But one evening in the late 1970s, as we lounged and chatted in our usual spots in the bedroom—John and Yoko on the bed, me in my white wicker chair—Yoko held up an old brass key and suggested we give it a try.

It unlocked apartment 71, just down the hall from John and Yoko's, and the only other domicile on their side of the Dakota's seventh floor. For as long as anyone could remember, it had been occupied by an elderly woman who almost never opened her door, never showed her face, and never had any visitors. In that way, she was the perfect neighbor for the Lennons, and yet, despite her ghostlike profile, John and Yoko had been obsessed with acquiring her apartment almost from the moment they moved into the Dakota. They wanted their corner of the seventh all to themselves, their own private sanctuary on New York's Upper West Side, so that there was never a danger of anyone they didn't know—or that Yoko's numerologists hadn't vetted—ever stepping off the elevator into their personal oasis.

And then, miracle of miracles—just before Thanksgiving, if I'm recalling correctly—there were rumors that the woman was finally ready to sell. Her apartment had not been listed—technically it wasn't yet on the market—but John and Yoko had learned that 71's owner was not at home. Where she had gone, and for how long, they couldn't be sure; they only knew that, right at that moment, she wasn't there. So, with Yoko leading the way, clutching that mysteriously obtained key, the three of us left 72 and all but tiptoed down the hallway to investigate just what was behind 71's always-closed door.

After Yoko unlocked the apartment, all we could see was darkness. John felt around the wall next to the entranceway until he finally found a light switch, which turned on a single floor lamp way on the other side of what revealed itself as a grand, dark-wood-paneled living room. Weirdly, there was almost no furniture in the place—just three overstuffed club chairs near a fireplace arranged around a simple wooden coffee table, as well as a few other random, scattered pieces. Either the woman had already begun moving out or she'd lived for all those decades a remarkably uncluttered life.

We slowly inched our way into the uncharted dwelling, taking in the sky-high ceilings and banks of heavily draped windows, mentally measuring the floor space—I guessed 3,000

square feet, insignificantly smaller than 72—until we found ourselves standing at the club chairs by the fireplace. Yoko sat down
first. John and I followed suit.

"It's important that this woman sell us this apartment," Yoko
announced as she rummaged through a small bag that she had
brought with her.

"Well, why not make her an offer?" I suggested.

"Yes, but before we make an offer, we have to find out the
best way to make that offer," Yoko went on, arranging the contents of her bag—a candle, some crystals, and a deck of tarot
cards—on the coffee table. "She doesn't know us. So we must find
a way of getting her to *want* to sell us the apartment; otherwise
she might sell it to someone else who makes a better offer, or
maybe will it to a relative."

"And how do you do that?" I asked. John looked like he was
curious about the answer to that question as well.

"Just watch," Yoko said.

She lit the candle, rubbed the crystals between her fingers
for a few minutes, then spent several long moments turning over
cards, studying them intensely. John and I watched in silence,
mesmerized by her mystical rituals. Finally, Yoko closed her eyes,
breathed deeply, then blew out the candle.

"Is it done, Mother?" John asked.

"Yes," she said, gathering up her cards and crystals. "It is
done."

We left, turning off the light and locking up behind us.

Two weeks later, I was back home in Laurel Canyon when

the red light started flashing. "Have you spoken to Mother yet?" John asked when I picked up the phone.

"No, why?"

"We got 71!"

"Really?" I said. "How?"

"It was the magic, Ellie. Mother's magic!"

It may very well have been the magic. Or else Yoko made an offer on the place that the seller simply couldn't refuse—a different sort of magic—but either way, the Lennons finally had the seventh floor all to themselves.

At first, John and Yoko left the apartment pretty much exactly as we found it when we snuck in for our reconnaissance visit. Except for an antique, bubble-topped Wurlitzer jukebox that Yoko had purchased for one of John's birthdays, as well as a Yamaha electric piano she had given him, they hardly added any furniture to it or decorated it in any way at all—until about a year later, that is, on a snowy New Year's Eve, as the 1970s turned into the 1980s. That's when John transformed apartment 71, for one evening only, into "Club Dakota," the most exclusive—and enchanting—nightspot in all of New York City.

I'll get back to that extraordinary, once-in-a-lifetime event in just a moment. But first, a few words about holidays at the Dakota—arguably the most Dickensian building in Manhattan—which were remarkable occasions in their own right.

As I've made more than abundantly clear, John and Yoko were not religious people. Spiritual, for sure, but hardly traditional believers. Still, they took Christmas seriously, if not as a holy day, then certainly as secular celebration, particularly after Sean was born. They always had a tree, for instance—a big one, usually an eight-footer, festooned with old-fashioned bulbs and colored lights and tinsel, just like you'd find on a Christmas card—which stood in the nook off the kitchen in John and Yoko's entertainment center. One year Yoko even went so far as to garnish the otherwise pristine white room with a holiday bauble: a single unadorned pine branch elegantly placed in a vase. It was, I suppose, her own postmodern deconstruction of a traditional Yule tree. Personally, I thought it was a tad understated but lovely nonetheless.

They did not generally host Christmas parties, but they did entertain in a manner of speaking. And though their guest lists were extremely limited, they could sometimes be filled with stunning surprises. I remember one year when Paul and Linda McCartney turned up at the Dakota for Christmas lunch. I'd never met either of them, and I'd been given no indication they were coming—I'd assumed John and Yoko and I would be spending the day alone with Sean. But here were the four of them—John and Paul and Yoko and Linda—together again for the first time in years.

I've often wondered why John and Yoko wanted me present for this moment; I was keenly aware at the time of how much of an outsider I was at this all-too-personal gathering. I suppose John and Yoko might have felt the presence of a stranger—to Paul and Linda—would provide some sort of buffer, keeping everyone on their best behavior. I don't know, and I never bothered to ask.

But I was certainly grateful to have been included in the experience, as awkward and even oddly anticlimactic as it ended up being.

The lunch didn't take place at the Dakota; we decided to eat at Elaine's on Eighty-Eighth Street and Second Avenue. But everyone congregated in the white room first, where Yoko and Linda immediately gravitated to each other and just started talking. Paul and John seemed very convivial at first. They seemed like they might have just bumped into each other a month before, like not much time had passed.

Soon after, we all descended to the lobby and then climbed into the McCartneys' chauffeured car for the drive across town to the Upper East Side. Elaine's at the time was the red-hot center of New York City high culture. Along with Woody Allen—who was practically the dining room's unofficial mascot—the place was always buzzing with glitterati. Norman Mailer, Leonard Bernstein, Michael Caine, Jacqueline Onassis, Luciano Pavarotti, Elaine Stritch, Tom Wolfe, Mario Puzo, Gay Talese—on any given day, it was packed with enough New York celebrities to fill an Al Hirschfeld mural. But even amid all those luminaries, John and Paul breaking bread together with their wives was beyond conspicuous. Every eyeball in the restaurant was trained on our table. It made for a very self-conscious meal.

Also, with all due respect to its late proprietor, Elaine Kaufman, the food from her kitchen was infamously unpalatable. Somehow, Elaine's could turn a basic dish like chicken parmigiana into a goopy soup; the scampi there was so overcooked, you'd need the Jaws of Life to pry the shrimp from the shell. After perusing the small-printed menu, nobody at our table could find anything they wanted to risk ordering.

"You know," Linda finally offered, "there's a great pizza place not far from here. Maybe they could deliver?"

I had a hunch this would be a social faux pas—but I was also quite certain Elaine wasn't going to eject John and Paul and their wives from her restaurant for any reason. I found a pay phone in the back and ordered a couple of pies. They were delivered to the kitchen, where they were removed from their cardboard boxes and decoratively placed on Elaine's own platters.

After lunch, we all returned to the Dakota, where I hoped the repartee might become somewhat more sparkling. Yoko and Linda paired off for a bit and chatted amiably—the two of them got along famously, bonded by the shared experience, perhaps, of being married to a Beatle—while John and Paul stood by the windows overlooking Central Park, watching as the afternoon sky turned a whiter shade of pale over Manhattan. They remained silent for long stretches, until awkwardness forced one of them to take a stab at conversation.

"Are you making any music?" Paul asked at one point.

"Well, you know, I play some stuff for me, but I'm not working on anything. Music isn't what's driving me at this point. It's all about the baby. What about you?"

"Oh, I'm always recording," Paul said. "I couldn't live without the music in me life."

Then, for a spell, they fell back into silence.

It seemed that these two rock 'n' roll behemoths, men who in their youth had all but defined the zeitgeist of the '60s—who had inspired an entire generation and redirected music's very destiny—were now, a mere decade later, struggling to find things to say to each other.

A part of me found it sad. But then, what was I expecting? Even the best of childhood friends eventually slip into separate lives. It's called growing up. Now they were just two old chums who no longer had all that much in common. It was unreasonable of me to presume that merely being in the same room together would somehow ignite the genius and energy of John and Paul's initial creative partnership.

Still, on the walk back from the Dakota to the Plaza that evening, as I passed all the glimmering Christmas lights and heard snippets of holiday melodies wafting out of the few restaurants and bars that were still open and serving, I couldn't help but think that history might have been made on this day.

"Are you making any music?" Paul had asked John.

What if John had said something like "No, but me guitar is in the next room. Let's sit down and make some . . ."

God only knows what classic Lennon-McCartney creation might have been born that afternoon.

OF course, above all else, John and Yoko were now parents, so Christmas for them, like for most other moms and dads, was largely about buying gifts for their child. Unlike most families, though, John and Yoko enjoyed almost unlimited resources, so Christmas shopping with the Lennons was in some ways a wholly unique experience. For instance, not many dads had the clout to keep FAO Schwarz open after hours before Christmas for a private last-minute spree.

The FAO Schwarz flagship location on Fifth Avenue and Fifty-Eighth Street shuttered its doors years ago, but in its heyday, it was one of the great wonders of Manhattan shopping, the Taj Mahal of toy stores. Outside its entrance, a platoon of greeters dressed as life-sized wooden soldiers, complete with red, brass-buttoned coats and fuzzy bearskin hats, stood guard to welcome visitors and help customers load bags into waiting cabs. Inside, every imaginable doll, puppet, game, and gadget was not only stacked in a small mountain on a display table but also laid out to play with, so that kids (and grown-ups) could sample the prospective purchase before bringing it home. With a store like that, who needed Santa Claus?

John, however, obviously couldn't just waltz into FAO Schwarz, especially right before Christmas Eve, when it was packed elbow-to-elbow with shoppers. But one year, when Sean was barely a toddler, John asked me to call the store and see if they could shut down for an hour or two so that he could do a little last-minute gift buying. Not surprisingly, the management was not crazy about the idea. Closing its doors in the middle of their busiest sales season so that one celebrity—even a former Beatle—could purchase a few thousand dollars' worth of presents was not smart business practice. But they did offer to let John into the store after its normal closing time.

I happened to be in New York that Christmas and joined John for his FAO Schwarz after-hours excursion. John was about thirty-eight at the time, but the minute we stepped through the door, he dropped about three decades. He literally became a kid again.

As part of the decorations, there was a giant toy train track suspended from the ceiling and snaking around the store—it must have been fifty yards long—with big, chunky Lionel loco-motives huffing and puffing along its rails.

"That! Let's get that!" John exclaimed the second he saw it.

"And where would you set that up in the Dakota?" I asked him. "The dining room?"

"Okay," he said, dejected. "Maybe not that."

John had a complicated childhood after being abandoned by his father, mostly being raised by his aunt, and losing his mother as a teen. I suspect his own childhood Christmases in Liverpool were not particularly merry. So, as a grown-up, he was clearly determined to compensate, and not just for his son's sake but for his own. John ended up buying thirty or forty toys at FAO Schwarz, all ostensibly for Sean but really things that mostly ap-pealed to him: electronic gadgets and games that his son was still way too young for but that would end up getting plenty of hours of playtime anyway. John would see to that.

As huge a haul as it was, though, those presents were only a fraction of the gifts that Sean would ultimately find waiting for him on Christmas morning. In the days and weeks before then, scores of packages would arrive for Sean from all over the world, with John and Yoko's friends falling over themselves to give offerings to the littlest Lennon. Literally, there must have been two hundred or more brightly papered and beribboned gifts spilling out from under the family Christmas tree, all with Sean's name on them.

At the Lennon household, by the way, Christmas morning started at exactly one minute past midnight. That's when John and Yoko would wake Sean, lead him to the tree, and let him tear open his gifts. I was there for several of those unboxings and there was always something of a tornado-like ambiance to the scene, with wrapping paper and cards flying all over the place. I would usually take it upon myself to try to keep track of who sent Sean what so that it would be easier to send thank-you notes to the correct givers. But it was a hopeless task, and eventually I would throw up my hands and let the mayhem unfold naturally.

Some of the presents were wildly age-inappropriate. Elton John once sent Sean a motorbike; Sean was too small to even sit on it. Many people sent stuffed animals, which he had zero interest in; he'd just toss those to the side. He did seem to like a chemistry set that someone had given him, although, again, Sean was too young to be mixing minerals and sulfurs. The one gift he seemed most attracted to, curiously enough, was a set of crystals. It was one of the few presents he actually took back to his room with him and kept at his bedside. Like mother, like son.

John and Yoko also gave each other gifts, of course. Some

were the traditional sort of trinkets wealthy spouses purchased for one another. Yoko once got John a wristwatch from Cartier. He once got her a white diamond necklace, the only piece of jewelry I'd ever seen the usually un-bejeweled Yoko wear. But sometimes they could be impressively creative in their gift giving, particularly John. One time he asked me for help in recording a musical tape as a present to Yoko. John and I sat in the white room, a cassette recorder next to him as he played "Stardust" on the white piano while, at his insistence, I sang the lyrics into the mic—although, to be truthful, "sang" might be a generous word for what came out of my mouth. Whatever meager talents I may possess in this life, singing is not one of them. When John played the tape of my crooning to Yoko, he recorded her reaction to my less-than-Willie-Nelson delivery and later played it back for me. I could hear Yoko say something like "Oh God, no! Please make it stop!" followed by peels of her laughter.

But by far the greatest Christmas gift John ever gave to Yoko—as well as to me—wasn't anything he'd purchased at a store or recorded onto a cassette tape. It was an event, an enchanted twinkling of pure distilled joy, that he orchestrated just for the three of us during the waning hours of December 31, 1979.

A few days earlier, John had laid out his plans to me. He wanted to turn the newly acquired apartment 71 into a private club. John was not a huge fan of nightlife—crowds were problematic for obvious reasons—but he enjoyed the concept of an exclusive, intimate space, something like an old English men's establishment. He'd read about John Belushi and Dan Aykroyd's private blues sanctum in Chicago and wanted to construct something like that for himself right there on the seventh floor of the Dakota. So, shortly after Christmas, he and I went shopping on New York's Lower East Side, where there were dozens of second-hand shops, and proceeded to purchase enough cheap furniture and other decorations—overstuffed sofas, martini shakers, pink flamingo cardboard cutouts—to turn 71 into what John had by now begun referring to as Club Dakota.

After furniture shopping, we spent a few hours combing through vintage record shops, looking for old 78s to fill that antique bubble-top jukebox Yoko had given John. (We found Dooley Wilson singing "As Time Goes By," Bobby Darin's "Dream Lover," Bing Crosby's "Please," Gracie Fields's "Sally," and scores more.) Then we headed to Canal Street and picked up moldy old black-tie tails and white gloves to wear on Club Dakota's opening night, which John had decided would be on New Year's Eve. Technically, John and I were to be the club's only charter members, but he instructed me to write out a formal invitation to Yoko, which I would later hand deliver to her on a silver platter. Yoko was made merely an "honorary" member because, as John joked to me, otherwise she would immediately try to sexually integrate the club.

I have thought often about that night, about how best to describe it to those who weren't lucky enough to be there (which, of course, would be the whole rest of the world). And the best I can come up with is that it was like spending a blissful interlude suspended in a magical snow globe. In my memory, we all seem to move in slow motion, as if gliding through glycerin-laced air. The three of us—Yoko in an elegant black evening gown, John and I in ridiculous old penguin suits (he paired his with a white T-shirt and his old Liverpool school tie)—danced and laughed (and smoked) together without a care in the world, the jukebox filling the living room with glorious old tunes from the '40s and '50s. I took dozens of Polaroid photos of them that night, but for some reason none of them capture the magic of the moment.

And then, at midnight, our reveries were interrupted by the pop and crackle of fireworks. We all stood by the windows and watched the skyline over Central Park light up with flaming balls and sparkling whirly fountains and a slew of other aerial bursts and barrages. I'd never seen anything more beautiful in my life. And I'd never seen John and Yoko looking more content and in love.

It was that rarest, most precious thing in life—a perfect moment.

It would also, as fate would have it, be John's last New Year's Eve.

He would be dead before the next one.

FIFTEEN

Los Angeles and the Dakota, 1980

A re you okay?"

I was surprised by the question. For starters, the person asking was my mother, who called me in Laurel Canyon from our old apartment in Washington Heights. We didn't speak often, certainly not at this hour, around 8:00 p.m. on the West Coast, 11:00 p.m. in her time zone. Unlike me, my mom was not a night owl.

"I'm fine," I told her. "Why do you ask?"

"Well, because I just heard on the radio that there was a shooting at that building on Seventy-Second Street that you're always visiting. I didn't know if you were in New York or Los Angeles. I wanted to make sure you were okay."

"I'm okay," I told her, but suddenly I wasn't. I knew that if a shooting in New York was being reported on local radio, the victim was likely somebody newsworthy. And the most news-worthy people I knew on Seventy-Second Street were John and Yoko.

I rushed my mom off the phone and immediately dialed the Lennons' apartment. There was no answer. I called the Studio One offices on the first floor of the Dakota. No answer. I called the front desk at the Dakota. No answer. I called the front desk again, and again, and again, until finally somebody picked up.

"Yes" is all he said—not hello, just "Yes." But I recognized the voice of the Dakota operator.

"It's Elliot Mintz," I said, knowing he knew my name. "Is everything all right over there?"

There were a few seconds of silence, then a dial tone. He'd hung up on me.

Now I was starting to panic. Something obviously was not all right.

I flipped on the television. This was 1980—Monday, December 8, 1980, to be precise—the year of CNN's launch but still a good decade before the full ascendance of the cable TV twenty-four-hour news cycle. All I found on the air was a football game and some sitcoms.

I made a snap decision. It wasn't very rational, not at all thought through—but something told me I needed to get to New York as quickly as possible. I threw some clothes into a bag, rode the hillevator down to the street, hopped in my car, and headed towards LAX. Like so many parts of the battered old Jag, the radio wasn't working, so I remained in a news blackout all the way to the airport. Once there, I barely had time to park, dash to the counter to buy a ticket, and run to the gate before the last take-off of the day—the 10:00 p.m. red-eye—closed its doors. But I made it just in time and settled into a seat near the nose cone, a section that was entirely empty except for me. The Monday night red-eye, it turned out, was not a particularly popular flight.

After the jet took off and lifted its wheels—and it was too late to change my mind—part of me started to wonder if perhaps I'd acted rashly. Checking the facts in my head, I realized I had no real actionable information about what was going on at the Dakota. My mother had heard a radio report about a shooting on Seventy-Second Street. The Lennons were not answering their phones, and neither were their offices. The Dakota operator had hung up on me. That's it. That was the sum total of what I knew for sure. Was that enough to send me racing to the airport to catch the last flight to New York? I started to suspect I may have overreacted.

But then I saw a flight attendant exit the cockpit, her face red and blotchy, her mouth quivering, tears streaming down her cheeks. In all my years of flying, I'd never witnessed anything like it. As she hesitatingly made her way down the aisle, I reached out and touched her arm.

"Are you okay?" I asked.

"They killed him," she answered, gulping back a sob. "They murdered John Lennon."

I don't know how it's possible, traveling at five hundred miles per hour, but suddenly everything around me seemed to freeze in midair.

The psychological term for what I experienced is "delayed emotional response." For a long moment I found it impossible to process what I'd been told. I understood the words the flight attendant had said to me, their meaning couldn't have been clearer, but my neural network seemed to have suffered some sort of system-wide failure, shutting down my capacity to comprehend. Instead, I numbly sat in my chair, my mouth slightly agape, and stared into the seat back in front of me, waiting for my mind to reboot.

And then, like a flash fire in the brainpan, the full unreal horror of what happened exploded in my consciousness. "John is dead," I whispered to myself. My best friend was gone. My heart began to race, I found myself gasping for air. I literally doubled over in pain as my whole body absorbed the shock. I felt lucky that the plane was so empty and no one could see me.

I don't know how long I sat there like that, crumpled in agony, but eventually I regained at least a modicum of composure and started to take inventory of my situation. I was stuck in an aluminum tube at 30,000 feet. Airlines hadn't yet introduced Airfones, and personal cells were still rare, so there was no way for me to communicate with the ground. As gutted as I was, I realized I had to marshal my thoughts and plan what to do once the plane touched down at JFK at six in the morning. I knew that the one thing I couldn't do was show up at the Dakota an emotional wreck. That wouldn't have helped anyone. I needed to pull myself together, bury my grief, and be strong for Yoko and Sean.

Easier said than done. For the next several hours, as I soared through the night sky, I did my best to absorb the unimaginable.

I had seen John just a few weeks earlier, in New York; he and Yoko and I had spent a long evening at the Dakota listening to their soon-to-be-dropped *Double Fantasy* album. They'd been toiling on it for several months at The Hit Factory, recording the fourteen songs—most of them odes to devotional love, a musical dialogue of sorts between the two of them—that would fill their most personal and, in some ways, passionate LP yet. Also, their last while John was alive, released just weeks before John's death.

I'd visited the studio three or four times on various trips to New York in the summer of 1980, and I was struck by how dramatically different the scene was from the raucous recordings six years earlier at the Spector Sessions in Los Angeles. It was a flawlessly professional operation. No drugs or alcohol were permitted on the premises. No junk food, either; Yoko had fresh sushi delivered at mealtimes and arranged trays around the studio filled with sesame seeds and other healthful, natural snacks (the only exception being the tins of biscotti cookies that John could not resist). I remember a large photograph of Sean, then five years old, taped to a video monitor over the sound mixing board. Also, there was a small, all-white anteroom off the listening area where an assistant named Toshi prepared and served tea. Yoko had decorated it as if re-creating their Dakota apartment in miniature. A few hundred square feet of home away from home.

The two of them had never looked more happy or fit. John had taken up swimming and was as lean and wiry as an athlete—

without the help of any fat-melting injections. Yoko was radiantly serene, more at peace with the world than I think I'd ever seen her.

I just happened to be in New York on the evening in mid-November when the first commercial release of the completed album was delivered, so they invited me back to the Dakota for an impromptu *Double Fantasy* listening party. The two of them lay on the bed with their heads propped up on pillows—the speakers of John's surprisingly mediocre stereo system were behind them on a mantelpiece—while I sat at the foot of the mattress. We listened to the album twice.

"So, tell me what you *don't* like about it?" John asked when it was over.

I just smiled. I thought it was a beautiful, extraordinary work, unlike anything the two of them had ever recorded before, and certainly unlike anything John had recorded as a Beatle. "I'll be here for a long time before I can come up with an answer to that question," I told him. "I can't think of anything I don't love about it."

At around two in the morning, after we'd talked some more, I could tell the two of them were growing weary, so I got up and said my goodbyes. John walked me to the door.

"You taking a cab to the Plaza?" he asked.

"I think I'd rather walk," I said.

"Remember," he cautioned me, "walk on the side of the street where the doormen are. Don't walk on the side of the street next to the park."

"John," I said, "I grew up in New York. I know how to walk in this city."

Over the next couple of weeks, John and I talked on the phone four or five times, maybe more, but that was the last time I saw him in the flesh, at the doorway of his home at the Dakota, where he was fretting over *my* safety on the very street where he would soon be slain.

When my plane landed at JFK, the first thing I did was find a pay phone and call John and Yoko's offices at the Dakota. This time I got through and was put on the line with Richie De Palma, Studio One's office manager, who sounded predictably distraught and exhausted. He gave me a few details about the shooting; at the time, they didn't know much, and, frankly, I wasn't ready to hear much more. I told him I was on my way from the airport and would be there in under an hour.

"There's a crowd here," he said. "I'll wait for you in front of the building and help get you in."

There was a crowd all right. By the time I got to the Dakota, at around 7:30 in the morning, at least 5,000 people had gathered on Seventy-Second Street, and more were arriving every moment. A lot of people had brought boom boxes and were playing John Lennon and Beatles songs as hundreds sang along. Some were laying flowers against the Dakota's towering iron gates. A few had made signs, which they held up almost as if attending a protest. One of them aptly read, "WHY?"

I saw Richie behind the barricades in front of the building and he waved me over. I elbowed through the crowd, not making much progress, until a couple of officers, at Richie's request, helped me across the police cordon. Suddenly, I was face-to-face with the crime scene, which had not yet been cleared: there was blood on the pavement—John's blood—as well as shards of broken glass from a window shattered by one of the bullets. For a second I was reminded of the night I saw Sal Mineo's dead body under a yellow tarp outside his apartment building in West Hollywood. I couldn't help but think that at least this time I was being spared a similar view. I seriously doubted I could have handled that again.

I rode the elevator to the seventh floor and knocked on apartment 72's door, still protected by those Tibetan bells hanging from the knob. The Lennons' longtime housekeeper, Masako, let me in. There were bags under her eyes; it was clear she'd been crying.

"Yoko-san in bedroom," she said in broken English. "Door locked."

I took the familiar steps down the hallway to the bedroom where I'd spent so many hours in conversation with John and Yoko. I paused at the closed door and took a moment to think about what I was going to do next. I felt enormous apprehension but was also relieved that I had composed myself enough so that when Yoko opened the door, I wasn't going to break out in tears. My goal was not to react—to follow her need. I took another breath and then I gently knocked.

"Yoko, it's Elliot," I told her softly. "I'll be right outside until you are ready to see me. I'm not going anywhere."

I sat down in the hallway and waited. I suppose I would have remained at that spot for hours, days if necessary. But after only about five minutes, I heard the lock click and saw the door open a crack. I stood up and peered inside the bedroom, illuminated by the big-screen TV, which was showing live local news footage of the Dakota. Yoko had been watching, with the volume off, for who knows how long. Even though the windows were shut and the shutters closed, I could hear the music from seven floors below. The sound of mourners on the street singing John's lyrics would fill the apartment for days to come.

Standing by the bed, wearing silk pajamas and a kimono, Yoko looked incredibly frail. I reached over and gingerly put my arm around her. She touched my face, then crawled back into bed and under the covers. It was incredibly strange. I had never been in the room with just Yoko before: John and Yoko had always been there together. This was their bedroom, their nest. But John . . . was not there. Yoko looked devastated, hollow, lost.

"Is there anything I can do?" I asked her.

"There's nothing anybody can do," she weakly responded.

"Have you eaten anything? Can I bring a cup of tea?"

"Elliot," she answered, "your presence is comforting. You don't have to say or do anything."

So I didn't. I sat down in my usual spot, the white wicker chair, and we both watched the images flickering on the TV. It was a bit odd to be inside the building that was being shown on the screen, to know that the cameras relaying these pictures of the throngs outside were just a hundred or so yards away. I took a moment to make sure the bedroom drapes were fully closed, concerned that a photographer with a telephoto lens—or, God forbid, someone with even more nefarious intentions—might be lurking in an apartment building across the street.

For a while, my eyes wandered around the room, eventually settling on John's bedside table, where I spotted a pile of books—what John was reading in what would turn out to be his final days. It was an eclectic stack, to say the least, everything from *The Second Sex* by Simone de Beauvoir to *Sugar Blues* by William Dufty to *The Anatomy of Swearing* by Ashley Montagu to *Your Child's Teeth: A Parent's Guide to Making and Keeping Them Perfect* by Stephen J. Moss. There was also a copy of *Mind Games*, Robert Masters and Jean Houston's seminal brain-training manual, as well as Ann Faraday's *The Dream Game*. I glanced to the other side of the bed and noticed Yoko's reading material, a similarly varied and fascinating selection of titles.

But then, suddenly, my attention was jolted back to the television. For the first time, a picture of the suspect appeared on the screen. Yoko sat up and stared intently at the mug shot of the assailant; she seemed both mesmerized and repulsed—and deeply confused—by the face of the man who, just hours earlier, had murdered her husband. I studied her eyes as she studied his. She appeared to be searching for something in the photo, undoubtedly the same thing that everyone around the Dakota—and around the world—had been searching for on this heartbreaking, dreadful day. She was looking for the answer to the question on that sign that was being waved outside in the crowd: "WHY?"

The following weeks were a blur. I spent a lot of them down-stairs at Studio One, joining a staff of four or five employees, fielding a never-ending barrage of phone calls. As soon as one of the five incoming lights went dark, another lit up. Many of the calls were from the press. Obviously, everyone wanted to talk to Yoko, but that was not going to happen. The last thing Yoko needed was to answer a bunch of questions in front of a micro-phone. The only press she did do was a brief taped video for Barbara Walters, who was impossible to say no to, even under the most arduous circumstances.

Not *all* the calls were from reporters, though. At one point early on, an assistant held out a phone for me. "He says he's Ringo Starr," she whispered, cupping the receiver with her palm. I took the handset. Turns out it *was* Ringo, who was calling from a pay phone and wanted to make a condolence call with his girlfriend (now wife), Barbara. I buzzed Yoko on the intercom, and she okayed Ringo's request. With the swelling crowds outside, get-ting them into the Dakota undetected was not an uncomplicated task; I ended up sneaking them into the building through a back entrance and up to the seventh floor in an old hand-cranked freight elevator.

"I know exactly how you feel," Ringo told her when she greeted him and Barbara in her bedroom.

"No, you don't," Yoko replied, "but I'm grateful you are here."

Eventually, Yoko would ask me to serve as official spokesper-son for the Lennon estate—she'd even pay me a small stipend—but at that moment I had no official job or title. I simply did whatever it was that needed to get done, and sometimes what needed to get done was the last thing I could have predicted.

One evening, just a day or two after John's murder, I returned to apartment 72 from answering calls downstairs to find Julian Lennon sitting alone in the kitchen. He was now seventeen and had just flown in from London by himself to pay his respects. (He told me later that the flight was filled with passengers reading papers covered with headlines about his father's killing.) John and Julian had made some repairs to their estranged relationship during the Lost Weekend, but Julian was still an outsider to the Lennon family. Despite the reunion in California, John and Julian continued to find it difficult to spend time together in the subsequent years. He had practically no relationship with Yoko or with his much younger half-brother, Sean.

"Would you look after Julian?" Yoko asked me when I stepped into her bedroom. She was still huddled under the covers, seeming to shrink a bit more every day. "It's so depressing here. Take him around New York, show him different places, make sure he isn't photographed."

She was asking partially as a kindness to Julian but also as a mercy to herself. Yoko was in no condition to deal with John's grieving teenage son; she could barely handle her own child's grief. Sean reminded her so much of John, she found it painful to be in the same room with him, so he and his nanny were dispatched to the Lennons' vacation home in Florida. I found the idea of sightseeing with Julian a bit odd—and, judging from his quizzical expression when I mentioned the idea, so did he. Nevertheless, we ended up spending a day together visiting Manhattan landmarks, culminating with a trip to the viewing deck atop the World Trade Center, which turned out to be one of the few pleasant interludes in an otherwise unbearable stretch of misery. For a brief second, Julian could see past the horizon.

The misery grew more and more unrelenting as the days and weeks rolled on—as did the stewing atmosphere of fear and dread inside the Dakota. Most ordinary families have the privilege of solitude during times of crisis, but the Lennons had never been ordinary. John's murder trained the world's attention on Yoko. The private sanctuary on the Dakota's seventh floor where she and her husband had once cocooned themselves had now been blown wide-open. Not only had Yoko's sense of safety and security been shattered—despite the presence of platoons of police outside and beefed-up private security inside—so, too, had any semblance of privacy. As well as decency.

John's body had been secretly transported to suburban Westchester for cremation. We learned afterwards that some despicable opportunist at the mortuary had photographed the corpse and sold the picture to the *New York Post* (which printed it in black and white on its front page) and the *National Enquirer* (which published it in grisly color). We heard that whoever took the picture had pocketed $10,000 for it, giving them the ghoulish distinction of being the first person to make a buck off John's death. They would hardly be the last.

One of the other assignments I took up around this time was reading through the bags of threatening letters that had been pouring into Studio One. John had obviously had a hugely posi-tive impact on millions of fans—in the coming days, some 200,000 of them would convene in Central Park to memorialize him on a patch of land that would soon be rechristened "Straw-berry Fields"—but there was a small subset within that popula-tion who were clearly deeply disturbed, and John's death seemed to have unleashed their toxic rage. I spent hours picking through hate mail—including a slew from a twisted "fan club" devoted to the killer, usually signed "Death to Ono"—separating them into various piles based on threat levels. The most worrying ones were flagged for further investigation by law enforcement and shared with Yoko's private security, who started pinning the names and descriptions of the senders on a bulletin board at Studio One, imploring the staff to raise an alarm should any of them be spot-ted near the Dakota. That bulletin board grew very crowded very quickly.

Bodyguards were regularly patrolling the residence. (Yoko spent more than a million dollars on private security in the year after John's murder.) I was always running into them in the kitchen, big, beefy-armed men, all off-duty police officers, in plainclothes jackets that barely covered their bulging shoulder holsters. The irony was impossible to miss: this house built on love and peace, this citadel of amity and harmony, was now filled with guns. Indeed, at one point, even I started carrying one. Yoko had asked me to help with her protection, particularly dur-ing the rare moments when the bodyguards were between shifts or stuck in traffic. And so I applied for and ultimately received a license for a concealed weapon—no easy task in New York City, even in 1980—and started carrying a snub-nosed .38 revolver in an ankle holster.

I was also provided with a bulletproof vest, which was so bulky and uncomfortable, I almost never wore it. In fact, one of the few times I recall willingly slipping into the flak jacket was when a man fitting the description of one of the assailant's fan club letter writers was spotted on the street outside the Dakota. It was one of those moments when a bodyguard was not available, so I ended up volunteering to investigate the suspect. He was a tall, young, otherwise innocuous-looking fellow. I approached him carefully and asked him for the time. When he lifted his wrist to look at his watch, I could see under his jacket what appeared to be the butt of a gun sticking out from his belt. I quickly returned to the Dakota lobby and called the police. They arrived in minutes, pushed him against a wall, discovered what was indeed a weapon, and hurried him away.

But nearly as shocking and upsetting as the dangers that were swirling outside the Dakota were the perils lurking inside. Sadly, heartbreakingly, over the next several months, Yoko would learn that she was surrounded by backstabbers, that some of her most trusted confidants were secretly—and sometimes not so secretly—scheming against her.

For starters, there's John Green, the "Oracle," as John nicknamed him, Yoko's favorite tarot card reader. Shortly after John's death, Green started running a scam at one of Yoko's downtown loft properties, charging admission to the public to examine the artworks and Beatles acetates that Yoko had been storing there—essentially running his own personal John Lennon Museum—until Yoko got wind of it and shut him down. Later, Green would publish a memoir, *Dakota Days*, in which he'd paint Yoko as a neurotic witch who had destroyed Lennon's talents.

There was also a security guard, a former FBI agent, named Doug MacDougall, whom Yoko at one point trusted to watch over Sean. When he quit after an incident at a playground—he left in a huff when Yoko admonished him for letting Sean out of his view—MacDougall called me to let me know he was holding some of John's old love letters to Yoko, as well as some of his eyeglasses, and would return them as soon as Yoko gave him several thousand dollars in what he called "back pay." She agreed, cut a check, and sent me to hand deliver it and pick up the purloined items.

But by far the worst offender, the most venomous in the Dakota snake pit, was an assistant named Fred Seaman. Fred wasn't just another Studio One staffer; he was the trusted aide who, earlier in the year, accompanied John on a trip to Bermuda—the trip on which John wrote many of the songs for *Double Fantasy*. Incredibly, almost immediately after the murder, Seaman began smuggling shopping bags stuffed with private papers from the Lennon offices and residences—including five personal journals that John kept hidden under his bed—hauling them uptown to the apartment of his accomplice, Robert Rosen, as part of a scheme they called "Project Walrus." They were planning to use the pilfered material to write a tell-all book about John in which

Seaman would portray himself as Lennon's true disciple, the one who really knew him best, better than even Yoko. In truth, it was a naked money grab: "Dead Lennons equal big $," as Seaman scrawled in his own diaries.

It took months—and, ultimately, the intervention of the Manhattan DA—but eventually we got the diaries back. And Seaman ended up pleading guilty to second-degree larceny. (One of the highlights of my life was that I got to write Seaman's confession.)

Not surprisingly, the toll all this took on Yoko was unbearable. As if losing her husband wasn't devastating enough, she found herself surrounded by traitors. Whom could she turn to? Whom could she believe? For a while, she leaned on the companionship of her friend and interior designer Sam Havadtoy, who not only moved into the Dakota but began sharing a bedroom with Yoko—not the one she slept in with John but another in the residence that she relocated to shortly after the murder. This struck many on her staff as curious, and not merely because it was so soon after John's death. Although Havadtoy was undeniably charming, appeared to have Yoko's best interests at heart, and was terrific with Sean, he was also a gay man. In fact, he left his boyfriend, a hairstylist named Luciano Sparacino, to move in with Yoko. Were he and Yoko lovers? I couldn't say. Only they could.

Despite the relationship and comfort she felt with Sam—whatever that relationship might have been—Yoko continued to grow more and more wary of just about everyone around her. It was understandable, I think, given the circumstances. But it turned life in the once-easygoing Dakota into something resembling a Kafka novel or a Kubrick thriller: a dark house of mirrors bubbling over with suspicion, paranoia, and gaslighting.

"Why is this happening to me?" Yoko asked at one point, distraught over the string of personal betrayals. "What did I do to deserve this?"

I had no answers. Because there were none.

I don't know if I ever fell under Yoko's suspicion—she never said anything to me to indicate as much—but I wouldn't be surprised. At a certain point, everyone in her orbit was suspect. I do recall one moment when Yoko and I came dangerously close to a serious argument, the first and only time in our friendship when I lost my cool with her.

News had leaked that Albert Goldman was planning a book about John. Goldman had been a well-respected journalist—a former *Life* magazine feature writer turned tell-all celebrity biographer—but he was also a serious threat. He'd already written bestselling bios of Elvis and Lenny Bruce that were devastating takedowns, and there was no reason to believe he would go easy on John and Yoko. On the contrary, we knew Goldman had been talking to Havadtoy's ex-boyfriend Luciano, as well as others who were not known to be big Yoko fans. Clearly, this was a hatchet job in the making.

As soon as it was published, our suspicions were confirmed. It was the most devastating portrait one could imagine—and it became an instant bestseller.

I implored Yoko to let me conduct a radio interview with her and Sean to dispel at least some of the more outrageous rumors being spun about the Lennon family, like the notion that John's "househusband" image was a public relations fraud; that he was an abusive husband and father (who once allegedly kicked Sean across a room); and that he was a drugged-out recluse, possibly schizophrenic, and an enthusiastic devotee of Thai prostitutes—along with a slew of other vile untruths.

"I've never asked you to comment about any of the other books, but this one we can't ignore," I told her.

Yoko paused for a moment, then responded. "Let me check with my advisors," she said, meaning her team of tarot readers and numerologists.

I'd never expressed skepticism about Yoko's mystical beliefs—after all, I had a few of my own—but the stakes after John's death were now so much higher. As valuable as these consultants may have been to Yoko, giving her mystical advisors so much power no longer appeared to me to make any sense, especially since their track record had not exactly been stellar. So, for once, I pushed back.

"Yoko, let me ask you something," I said. "If these advisors are as good as you believe they are, why is it that none of them saw what was going to happen to John? Why was there no warning? How could they miss that?"

Yoko's answer astonished me.

"Elliot," she said, "how do you know I wasn't warned? Did you ever ask me if there were warnings?"

"Well, no, I just assumed—"

"No, don't use that word," she interrupted. "You know I don't like that word."

"Okay," I said, trying very hard to stay composed, "I'll ask you: Did any of your advisors warn you about John being in danger?"

"Yes," she answered. "I was told he was in danger in New York and that he should be removed immediately. That's why I sent him to Bermuda over the summer. All this time I've been saying I sent him so he could be inspired to write songs for *Double Fantasy*. That's the truth, but not the whole truth. I also sent him so he'd be out of Manhattan. But I couldn't keep him away forever. He had to come back at some point."

I was speechless.

"Look, Elliot," Yoko went on, "you know how John felt about his own safety. We talked about this at our kitchen table when your friend was killed. John said, 'If they're going to get you, they're going to get you.' It didn't matter what my advisors told me. He didn't believe in bodyguards, he wouldn't put up with them. He wanted to be free. He loved his freedom. What else could I do?"

The Dakota, 1981

I have found another pair of John's eyeglasses. This makes twenty-seven, and I add them to the inventory, along with all the other belongings I have been unearthing—the scores of Polaroid selfies, the Beatle costume in the closet, the sketchbooks full of doodles—as I continue my sweep of the Dakota apartments and the storage units of the building's dungeon-like basement. There are moments during this gloomy excavation of my dead friend's belongings, this grim accounting of John's material coil, that make me feel more alone and lost than I've ever felt before.

It's a brutal, dreadful endeavor, and yet I throw myself into it with everything I've got.

It may not be entirely conscious, but I suspect one of the reasons I plunge so vigorously into this and all the other chores

Yoko has asked me to perform—sifting through the hate mail, dealing with the press, working with her security team and spiritual advisors—is that I'm hoping it will distract me from the wrenching sorrow. If I don't allow myself the space to grieve—if I fill every second with activity, no matter how difficult or morbid—perhaps I can keep the pain at bay.

It doesn't work. Because as I riffle through John's drawers and rummage through his cabinets, I inevitably come across items that send me reeling into the past, summoning memories that break my heart over and over again.

In a cardboard box on a shelf, I find an old acetate of *Some Time in New York City* and I'm instantly transported back to Ojai and my first in-person meeting with John and Yoko. I remember how excited they were when they presented me with the just-finished album—and how hard they laughed the next day when I told them I'd been fired for playing it on my radio show.

In a drawer, I find a bag full of old photographs, including a snapshot of John and me on the beach at Big Sur, passing a fat joint between us, before we all piled back into the Dragon Wagon and tore up the Pacific Coast Highway to San Francisco, Little Eva's "The Loco-Motion" blaring at full volume on John's crazy mobile stereo system.

In a pile of clothing in the basement, I find the moldy old penguin jacket John wore over a white T-shirt and school tie just a year ago at Club Dakota's opening (and closing) night. The cardboard flamingo cutouts we purchased for the event are leaning in a corner, remnants of a magical New Year's Eve spent inside our own enchanted snow globe.

And then, while poking around another room, I stumble upon something that will take my breath away. It's an envelope inside an innocuous-looking large brown file folder that I find inside some black steel cabinets half-hidden under a pile of art deco lamps and statues and an old harmonium that Allen Ginsberg must have left behind during a visit to the Dakota. The envelope is sealed, but I can tell from the handwritten address on the front that it's a letter from John, who obviously never got around to mailing it.

The name of its recipient is "Elliot Mintz."

I stare at it for a very long time.

I'm curious about its contents, of course—frankly, I'm wildly intrigued by the possibilities of what's inside—but something is keeping me from opening it. If John had wanted me to read it, I figure, he would have mailed it to me—or, more likely, had an assistant mail it for him—rather than leave it in a cabinet.

But there is a riddle I need to solve, and maybe, just maybe, there are clues inside this envelope.

Now that he's gone, I have of course been thinking a lot about my relationship with John as well as Yoko (with whom I have remained close in the years since) and how much they both meant to me. But also, frankly, how much they both required from me. I'm asking myself the question that will haunt me for the rest of my days: Was what I gave up for John and Yoko worth what I received in return? To paraphrase the final line of the final song on the Beatles' final studio album: In the end, was the love they took equal to the love they gave?

There's another question haunting me as well, one that will also trail me for the rest of my life: Of the three billion people alive on the planet in the early 1970s, why on earth did John and Yoko decide to befriend a young radio broadcaster in Laurel Canyon? Why did they make this unlikely former stutterer and chronic insomniac their closest and most trusted confidant?

Why *me*?

I have a working theory.

"John grows disappointed by almost everyone he meets," Yoko once warned me, and I think I now know why. Just about everyone who met John and Yoko saw them as "John and Yoko," the most famous rock 'n' roll couple in history. They were pop culture demigods—living, breathing icons—the ex-Beatle in tinted glasses and his avant-garde artist wife. Most people had a hard time seeing beyond that.

But I didn't. My job interviewing celebrities had made me fame-blind, all but incapable of being starstruck, so I saw John and Yoko without any quotation marks. I was, of course, aware of their eminence, and I was always deferential to their accomplishments and their status as once-in-a-century artists, but to me they were very much human beings, as flawed and complicated as the rest of us. And I think John and Yoko liked that about me. I think that's maybe what attracted them, the fact that they could be themselves with me. As rock 'n' roll gods, they were surrounded by worshippers. A real friend was much harder for them to find. And somehow they correctly intuited that I would be a real friend.

Of course, had I not plucked Yoko's *Fly* album from that stack of new releases in September 1971 and called her for that first radio interview, we may never have become friends at all. That moment sealed my fate, sent me inexorably on the path that would come to define my life.

And that raises yet another question: If I had made a different choice—if I had pulled a different album from that pile— what sort of life would I have ended up living? Would I have had a wife and family of my own? Or would I have had a smaller life, maybe as a lonely local DJ, spending my years toiling at some shoddy regional station, playing golden oldies to a handful of late-night listeners somewhere in the middle of nowhere. It could have turned out that way as well.

I made the choices that seemed right at the time—the choices that sometimes seemed impossible and hard. But at other times, there was so much joy—from the first trip up the California coast to "join the circus," the trip to Japan, eating turtle soup out of a shell, sitting next to John at the piano where he played "Imagine," meeting Sean and feeling like I'd finally found a real family. . . .

Would I have done anything differently? At the time, I couldn't possibly have predicted that John would be snatched away when he was forty; I fully expected that the three of us would grow old together. In retrospect, I was just fortunate to have shared nine years with these two extraordinary beings.

So, I stare at John's unmailed envelope for a while longer, pondering its contents, and then slip it back into the file cabinet.

I decide not to open it. That way, the conversation will never be over.

FORTY-ONE years after John's death, I find myself on Hollywood Boulevard watching the premiere of Peter Jackson's documentary *Get Back*, about the *Let It Be* sessions. As I sit there next to Julian, Sean, and Sean's girlfriend, Charlotte, I am filled with an incredible sense of emotion, and not a few tears, seeing John's face again, digitally restored and enhanced so he—and Yoko— appear almost exactly as they were fifty years ago.

I think of all the years since John died. Even after those first few remarkably intense months and years, Yoko and I kept up an almost constant, continuing conversation. Yoko needed me more after John's death, and I also became an employee, and the official spokesman for the estate.

Sean became a bigger part of my life as well. Even in the early days, before Sean could walk or talk, I could see the incredible love between the three of them. Once he started talking and being more animated, I grew very fond of him as his own person. And as he grew older, I felt more and more like a real part of the family. I remember sitting in the Dakota guest bedroom with Julian and Sean, who were both playing and laughing, and it just filled my heart. It was the kind of interaction and love I never achieved with my own family. I lived the most joyous parts of my life at the Dakota with John, Yoko, and Sean.

That night, as I looked at Sean, laughing, talking, and remembering, it struck me—while the similarities with his father are there for all to see, it's important for me to resist the urge to think of Sean as a little John Lennon. I have to disassociate my relationship with him from my relationship with his father. If I don't, that would be a disservice to Sean. I was always aware of this, but I didn't want to make a big deal about it—yet in many ways, Sean has become the embodiment of his father. He is going about the business of finishing his father's mission, and doing so without a lot of personal fanfare. And most significantly, no mother has ever had a child who watches over her with so much care and love and presence. It is an ongoing inspiration.

As for Yoko, she would tell me, even today, that she's not a very sentimental person. Every year, she would send out her Christmas and Happy New Year cards and give gifts. I remember when Yoko sent me an original art piece she made—a glass box with a glass key inside. A few weeks later, there was an earthquake and the key broke. I told her, and she said, "Don't worry." Within days, she sent me a new key and a note reading, "Keep the old key in the box, even though it's broken. But keep this one nearby."

Writing this, I remember that shortly after my first interview with John, he told me about an art exhibition he and Yoko were going to be part of in Syracuse, New York, at the Everson

Museum of Art. I asked him to tell me more about the exhibition. He said, "Yoko is doing a series where we're asking friends of ours to find something, something physical, of their essence, and send it to us, so Yoko can display it as part of the piece." I replied, "If I had some time, I would send you some audio recording tape, snip it up, and have you add it to the exhibit." He got tremendously excited. "You must do that. You must be part of this. Can you get it to us by tomorrow?" But there was no way to send it that quickly in those days, and I never got to contribute.

So maybe that is why I'm writing this now—these are my pieces of audiotape—fragments in the larger, unforgettable piece of art that is and was John's and Yoko's lives. Fragile and imperfect, but it's a contribution I send with my whole heart, as part of the conversation that I, too, wanted to go on forever.

ACKNOWLEDGMENTS

The writing of a book is, unsurprisingly, an endeavor that requires a seemingly endless team of people to turn an idea or, in my case, a lifetime of experiences, into a book suitable for public consumption. I have many people to thank for their roles in bringing *We All Shine On* onto the page and into the world.

My agent, Erin Malone at WME, who advocated tirelessly for this book from the very start. My editor, Jill Schwartzman, whose endless patience and careful attention ushered it into existence. Ben Svetkey, who helped me wade through my memories and string them along a narrative thread. The team at Dutton: John Parsley, Alice Dalrymple, Sarah Thegeby, Amanda Walker, Stephanie Cooper, Charlotte Peters, Erika Semprun, Lorie Pagnozzi, Kristin del Rosario, and Vi-An Nguyen. The gifted copy editors and proofreaders, David Chesanow, Katie Hurley, and Kate Griggs. My wonderful UK editor, Bill Scott-Kerr, and the team at Transworld, including Nicole Witmer, Sally Wray, Cat

Hillerton, Louis Patel, Hannah Winter, Rosie Ainsworth, Holly McElroy, and Phil Lord.

Karla Merrifield, the Studio One archivist. The Lennon Estate, Jared Geller, and Jonas Herbsman, whose knowledge and graciousness made this project possible.

Chip Madinger and Madeline Bocaro, whose eagle-eyed reads and deep knowledge on all things John and Yoko were invaluable.

Diana Fitzgerald, my longtime friend and attorney.

Fabrocini's restaurant and Dale Gresch, without whom I would have starved while writing this book.

Stephen Peebles, Simon Hilton, Scott Raile, Farshad Arbabi, Katherine Pegova, Jimmy Steinfeldt, Connor Monahan, Bob Gruen, Lee Stapleton, and Ms. Saimaru.

And, of course, Sean, Yoko, and John, whose impact on my life has been larger than I can express in any number of words, on any number of pages.

INDEX

INDEX

ABOUT THE AUTHOR

ELLIOT MINTZ is a professional media consultant who has worked with the likes of John Lennon, Yoko Ono, Bob Dylan, Paris Hilton, Diana Ross, and many others. Prior to being a consultant, Mintz worked as a radio DJ and television host and served as the entertainment correspondent for *Eyewitness News* on KABC.